Colin Spe[...]

Dales Way

the Complete Guide

2016
Published by Skyware Ltd.

Published in 2013 by
Skyware Ltd.
48 Albert Avenue, Saltaire, Shipley BD18 4NT
www.skyware.co.uk

ISBN 978 0 9559987 7 5

Revised and reprinted 2016.

*First published by Skyware Press 2011. Originally published by Dalesman Publishing
Company Ltd. 1970, 1973, 1976, 1979, 1983, 1987, 1994, 1995, 2002.*

Text © Colin Speakman 2013
Route maps © Tony Grogan 2013

British Library Cataloguing-in-Publication Data.
A catalogue record for this book is available from the British Library.

Every care has been taken in the preparation of this book and all the information has been
carefully checked and is believed to be correct at the time of publication. However, the
countryside changes and neither the author nor the publishers can accept responsibility
for any errors or omissions or for any loss, damage, injury or inconvenience resulting from
the use of this book.

PHOTOS: *Front cover - River Wharfe near Hubberholme; back cover - Upper Dentdale
near Cow Dub; title page - River Wharfe near Bolton Abbey.*

Printed by Briggs Bros. (Silsden) Ltd, Cononley Business Park, Cononley, West Yorkshire.

Contents

Contents 3

Overview map & key 4

Introduction 5

Dales Way Planner...**6**; Some practical points...**10**; The People's Path - how it all began...**13**; Ilkley...**17**.

Stage One: ILKLEY TO BARDEN 19

*Ilkley to Addingham...***20**; *Addingham to Bolton Abbey...***21**; Addingham...**22**; The Boy of Egremond...**23**; *Bolton Abbey to Barden Bridge...***24**; Bolton Priory...**26**; Barden Tower...**27**; The Yorkshire Dales National Park...**29**.

Stage Two: BARDEN TO GRASSINGTON 31

*Barden Bridge to Burnsall...***32**; Appletreewick...**33**; *Burnsall to Grassington...***36**; Grassington...**38**.

Stage Three: GRASSINGTON TO BUCKDEN 39

*Grassington to Conistone Dib...***40**; Kettlewell...**41**; Lead mining in Upper Wharfedale...**42**; *Conistone Dib to Kettlewell...***44**; *Kettlewell to Birks Wood...***46**.

Stage Four: BUCKDEN TO GEARSTONES 47

*Birks Wood to Yockenthwaite...***48**; *Yockenthwaite to Outershaw...***49**; Hubberholme...**50**; *The Upper Wharfedale Estate...***51**; Cam Fell High Road...**51**; *Outershaw to Cam Houses...***52**; *Cam Houses to Gearstones...***53**; The Dales Rail Story...**54**; Tom's Pennine Way and Mary's Pennine Bridleway...**56**. The Dales High Way...**56**.

Watershed Alternative 57

*Cam Houses to Wold Fell via Newby Head...***58**; *Wold Fell to Lea Yeat...***59**.

Stage Five: GEARSTONES TO SEDBERGH 60

*Gearstones to Dent Head...***61**; Artengill Viaduct...**62**; Dent Station...**63**; *Dent Head to Little Town...***64**; *Little Town to Dent...***65**; Dent and its Terrible Knitters...**67**; *Dent to Brackensgill...***69**; Sedbergh...**71**.

Stage Six: SEDBERGH TO BURNESIDE 72

*Brackensgill to Lincolns Inn Bridge...***73**; Brigflatts and Firbank Fell...**74**; *Lincolns Inn Bridge to Lowgill...***76**; *Lowgill to Beck Houses...***78**; *Beck Houses to Garnett Folds...***79**; James Cropper plc...**80***; Garnett Folds to Burneside...***81**.

Stage Seven: BURNESIDE TO BOWNESS-ON-WINDERMERE 83

*Burneside to Staveley...***84**; *Staveley to Hag End...***85**; The Lake District National Park...**86**; *Hag End to Bowness...***88**; Windermere...**91**.

THE DALES WAY LINK ROUTES 92

The Leeds Link 93

The Bradford Link 99

The Harrogate Link 105

Harrogate...**106**; The Battle for Haverah Park...**107**.

References, Photo credits & Acknowledgements 111

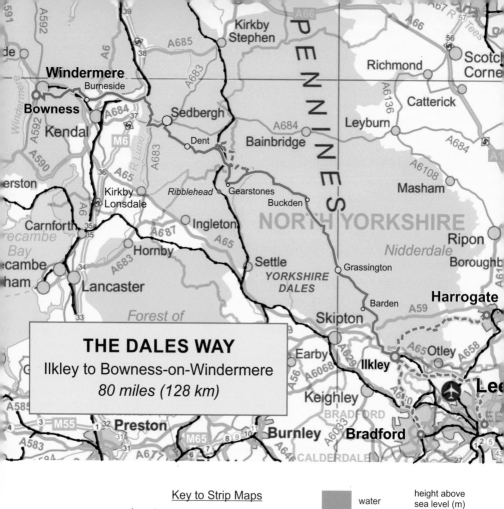

THE DALES WAY
Ilkley to Bowness-on-Windermere
80 miles (128 km)

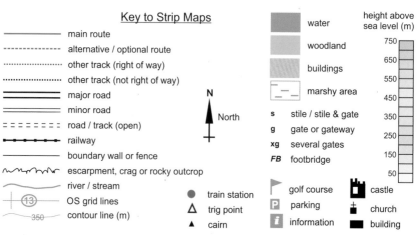

Maps based on OS 1: 25,000. Grid squares at 1 km (0.6 miles). Some details are exaggerated for clarity. Numbers in margins by main text refer to relevant map.

Introduction

The Dales Way is one of Britain's best loved, most written about, most popular, and as many people would argue, most beautiful long-distance walks.

It links urban West Yorkshire with the Lake District National Park, but in so doing completes a spectacular southeast-northwest traverse through the heart of the Yorkshire Dales National Park. This 80 mile route starts from Ilkley, on the edge of the West Yorkshire conurbation, and ends at Bowness-on-Windermere, the town on the shore of England's largest natural lake. Along the way it explores three of the main Yorkshire Dales – Wharfedale, including its major tributary Langstrothdale, Dentdale and Lunesdale.

Once outside the Yorkshire Dales, the Dales Way climbs out of the Lune Gorge below the Howgill Fells, over the valleys of the little rivers Sprint and Mint, then alongside the River Kent, before winding through the foothills of the Lake District, with some entrancing views of the high Lakeland fells before twisting down to the shores of Windermere itself.

But there's even more to the Dales Way. Unique among UK long-distance paths, it leads from the centre of two major cities, Leeds and Bradford, into two national parks, by continuous waymarked footpath. The Dales Way Leeds Link starts from Woodhouse Moor, less than a mile from the city centre, following a 20 mile route through an attractive green corridor via the Meanwood Valley, Adel Woods, Bramhope, and Otley Chevin to Ilkley.

The Bradford Link uses a 12 mile route from Bradford via industrial Bradford Dale, then through the world heritage site of Saltaire, across Bingley and Ilkley Moors to the start of the main Dales Way.

The newest Dales Way link is the 16 mile route from Harrogate. This starts from Valley Gardens close to the town centre, past Harlow Carr, winding through Haveragh Park, the Washburn Valley, and over Denton Moor to Ilkley.

Approaching Outrun Nook

DALES WAY PLANNER

PLACES (Italics - Offroute)	Distance from last miles (km)	Total distance miles (km)	Pub	B&B	Shop	Café food drink	Bus train	Camping bunkhse hostel	Facilities
ILKLEY	0	0	✓	✓	✓	✓	✓		T P C
ADDINGHAM	2.7 (4.3)	2.7 (4.3)	✓	✓	✓	✓	✓		T P
BOLTON BRIDGE	2.6 (4.2)	5.2 (8.4)	✓	✓		✓	✓		P
BOLTON ABBEY	0.8 (1.3)	6.0 (9.7)		✓	✓	✓			P
CAVENDISH PAV.	1.0 (1.6)	7.0 (11.3)			✓	✓			T P
STRID CARPARK	1.3 (2.1)	8.4 (13.5)			✓	✓	✓		T
BARDEN	0.9 (1.4)	9.3 (15.0)					✓	✓1	
HOWGILL	1.4 (2.3)	10.7 (17.2)	✓						
APPLETREEWICK	1.1 (1.8)	11.8 (19.0)	✓	✓			✓	✓	P
BURNSALL	1.2 (1.9)	13.0 (20.9)	✓	✓	✓	✓	✓		T P
HEBDEN			✓	✓	✓	✓	✓		P
GRASSINGTON	3.2 (5.1)	16.2 (26.1)	✓	✓	✓	✓	✓		T P C
CONISTONE									P
KETTLEWELL	6.2 (10.0)	22.4 (36.0)	✓	✓	✓	✓	✓	✓	T P C
STARBOTTON	2.2 (3.5)	24.6 (39.6)	✓	✓			✓	✓	P
BUCKDEN	2.2 (3.5)	26.8 (43.1)	✓	✓	✓	✓	✓		T P
HUBBERHOLME	1.2 (1.9)	28.0 (45.1)	✓	✓					
YOCKENTHWAITE	1.5 (2.4)	29.5 (47.5)		✓					
BECKERMONDS	2.2 (3.5)	31.7 (51.0)		✓				✓	
OUTERSHAW	1.1 (1.8)	32.8 (52.8)		✓2				✓2	
CAM HOUSES	3.1 (5.0)	35.9 (57.8)							
GEARSTONES	2.9 (4.7)	38.9 (62.6)							
RIBBLEHEAD			✓	✓			✓	✓	
COWGILL	5.2 (8.4)	44.1 (71.0)	✓	✓			✓	✓	
DENT	4.2 (6.8)	48.3 (77.7)	✓	✓	✓	✓		✓	T P
BRACKENSGILL	3.2 (5.1)	51.5 (82.9)		✓3					
SEDBERGH	1.7 (2.7)	53.2 (85.6)	✓	✓	✓	✓	✓		T P C
LINCOLNS INN BRG	3.6 (5.8)	56.8 (91.4)		✓2,3					
LOWGILL	3.6 (5.8)	60.4 (97.2)							
GRAYRIGG	2.9 (4.7)	63.3 (101.9)					✓	✓2	
PATTON BRIDGE	2.2 (3.5)	65.5 (105.4)		✓3				✓2	
A6	2.0 (3.2)	67.5 (108.6)		✓3					
BURNESIDE	1.6 (2.6)	69.1 (111.2)	✓	✓	✓		✓		T P
KENDAL			✓	✓	✓	✓	✓	✓	T P C
BOWSTON	0.9 (1.4)	70.0 (112.7)		✓					
STAVELEY	2.3 (3.7)	72.4 (116.5)	✓	✓	✓	✓	✓		T P
HAG END	3.6 (5.8)	75.9 (122.1)							
BOWNESS	2.7 (4.3)	78.6 (126.4)	✓	✓	✓	✓	✓	✓3	T P C

NOTES: (1) - Group bookings. (2) - Nearby on route. (3) Nearby off route. T - toilets. P - phone. C - cash machine
For guidance only, the details are subject to change. Please check with the Dales Way Association website.
Start and end points at Dales Way benches. Add distances to start and finish points, expect to walk 80 miles at least.

So why spend several days walking between West Yorkshire and the Lake District – or indeed between the Lake District and West Yorkshire as some people do, when you could drive the same distance in a couple of hours?

Walking for leisure is an activity which has a relatively recent history, and then only in the more prosperous parts of the world where walking in terms of transport is no longer a necessity.

The popularity of leisure walking only goes back to the late 18th and early 19th century, a time of rapid industrialisation and the growth of factories, mines and industrial cities, especially in the north and midlands of England. A group of writers we now define as English Romantic poets and essayists saw walking as a way of reconnecting with the natural world, especially with the mountains and lakes of Cumbria, the Highlands and Snowdonia and in later years the Alps. Prime among the walker-poets was William Wordsworth who had a massive, enduring influence not only among the next generation of writers and artists, but among philosophers, philanthropists, social reformers, and eventually campaigners for the countryside, footpaths, access, open spaces and national parks.

It is especially fitting therefore that the Dales Way connects the former industrial areas of the old West Riding with that most iconic landscape of the Romantic movement, where many ideas about the countryside and national parks were born - the Lake District.

But in so doing, it passes through a landscape which in its way has become equally iconic, not so much for the natural splendours of mountains and lakes as for a landscape which contains a rare harmony between man and nature: the wild, open fell country of the central Pennines, with its wind scoured summits and gritstone outcrops, limestone crags, caves and waterfalls; and the intimate cultivated pastoral valleys, dominated by scattered villages and farmsteads, miles of dry stone walls and barns. The Yorkshire Dales is a cultural landscape reflecting a pastoral economy which goes back over 4,000 years to Bronze and Iron Age times, to Roman and later Anglo-Saxon settlement, to the great medieval sheep walks created by the monasteries, and above all to a post-monastic and early industrial landscape of small enclosures, water-powered mills and mill communities, and lead mining villages. In some places it is a leisure landscape, old hunting forest, parkland and even romantic walks created by families whose wealth lay in early industry and commerce.

The walker, uniquely, has time to absorb all these influences and shaping forces. On foot you begin to rediscover the true scale of a landscape so diminished by hyperactive, high-speed modes of travel. Unlike passengers within the protecting shell of a car, the walker is exposed to the elements and all his or her senses are engaged. The Dales Way gives the walker ample time and space to understand and appreciate the many subtle forms and colours, effects of light, time of day and season, on riversides and fell tops, the rich variety of the natural world, plants, bird and small mammals. Walking is about reconnecting with the real world.

Long-distance walkers who have been able to enjoy several days following a continuous route enjoy these benefits in abundance. Short circular strolls back to the security of a car, whilst welcome, never really shake off that psychological umbilical cord, that invisible chain which draws you back to that little bit of urban living. True freedom is to stride out, for days on end, with a real sense of purpose, which Germans call *Zielwanderung*, or destination walking. There is perhaps no finer way of understanding the scale and complexity of a landscape and personal satisfaction in achieving that goal than to

Path near Cleabarrow on the final stage

walk to somewhere special, the 21st century equivalent of a pilgrimage.

So what better destination than the Lake District, one of England's most beautiful national parks, where the romantic passion for long distance walking began? But along the Dales Way you do so by experiencing that other very different, but equally beautiful, national park, the Yorkshire Dales. It is possible to escape, at least for a few days, from many of the pressures and frustrations of modern living, but more important in that escape to enjoy a rich, complex and pleasurable experience and physical activity which really does change, in subtle but important ways, the kind of person you are.

Walking the Dales Way is therefore a very special kind of experience that for over 40 years, increasing numbers of people, and indeed new generations, have come to share.

Upper Wharfedale

Bolton Abbey Estate
on the first stage

Some practical points

Unlike many long-distance routes, you don't have to be super-fit to walk the Dales Way. There are no steep hills – though at least one long and steady climb. It's more of a family walk to be taken at a moderate or even gentle pace, whatever your age and physique. But a reasonable standard of fitness is required – you need to be able to walk up to about fifteen miles, with a loaded rucksack.

You can backpack along the route, staying at B&Bs, village inns and guesthouses – though only one youth hostel, at Kettlewell, remains on the route. Camping is a little more difficult, as there are few campsites, but several farms along the Dales Way now offer bunkhouse barns which provide basic but clean and comfortable accommodation. Because of the popularity of the Dales Way, accommodation can get fully booked in the summer months, and advance booking is essential. Another tip is to avoid starting the route on a Saturday from Ilkley; if everyone heads north at the same time then all accommodation will be booked up.

The Dales Way Association website - **dalesway.org** - includes details of accommodation, from campsites and bunkhouses to comfortable bed and

breakfast establishments and country house hotels. The website also gives information about any path changes or diversions, services and facilities, and a very useful public transport guide. Please note that the former printed Dales Way Handbook, which was produced jointly with the Ramblers Association, has now been discontinued.

Alternatively you can do the walk in day stages, ending your day's hike in time to get

the bus or train back to Ilkley or a waiting car. A good compromise is to stay two or three nights in your chosen accommodation and to use local buses to access the route. This is very easy along the links from Leeds, Bradford or Harrogate to Ilkley, and also on the first three day stages between Ilkley and Buckden, served by the Upper Wharfedale bus.

Beyond Buckden more planning is required – you could for example use the Settle-Carlisle railway from Ribblehead or Dent. Further north between Sedbergh and across the Lune, Sprint and Mint valleys, where none of the rural bus services run on a Sunday, careful pre-planning is needed. However, frequent rail and bus services at the Burneside, Staveley and Windermere end of the walk make for easy day stages and excellent return transport.

Thanks to some good waymarking – look for the distinctive Dales Way waymark - path finding on the Dales Way is now much easier, especially in the southern sections, though it can be tricky in the quieter northern sections. Good maps are essential - those in this book may be supplemented with OS Outdoor Leisure 1:25,000 series.

Always have emergency supplies of food and especially drink with you (remember mobile phones do not function in many parts of the Dales). A decent pair of boots is essential along the Dales Way – even if the weather is dry, paths are often muddy and wet. Have waterproofs and a spare sweater in the rucksack at all times – weather in the hills can change with

surprising speed. Insect repellent and a sun hat are also essential in the summer months.

Finally remember the Dales Way goes through a working countryside, where farmers need to earn a living. Always act sensibly and thoughtfully. If you have a dog keep it on a lead as there is almost always livestock about. There have been isolated incidents even on the Dales Way when cattle, alarmed by dogs, have attacked walkers. Never walk between a cow and its calf, and in an emergency let go of the dog – it can look after itself better than you can. Always close gates behind you unless obviously propped open, keep to public rights of way or clearly indicated permissive paths and access areas, and take all litter back home. That way you will be always welcome in the countryside.

(Above) Fleur and Colin Speakman, who first surveyed the route of the Dales Way in 1969, are here shown sitting on the newly installed Dales Way seat at the finishing point above Bowness, 1993.

(Below) Dales Way Association members arrive at the viewpoint near Grandsire, with the Lakeland Fells in the distance, on the final leg of the Dales Way.

The People's Path – how it all began

the dales way

When in 1968 the Countryside Act gave local authorities new powers to create public access to riversides, members of the West Riding Area of the Ramblers Association saw it as a heaven-sent opportunity to create public access to several popular riversides in the Yorkshire Dales. But discussions with senior planning officers of the old West Riding county council suggested that there would be more chance of success if just one riverside was prioritised.

The obvious choice was the River Wharfe. The Ramblers therefore decided to seek a through walking route along the Wharfe from Ilkley on the edge of the Leeds-Bradford conurbation.

But ending a walk somewhere near the river's source high on Cam Fell, where the Wharfe oozes from tiny streamlets in a boggy waste, didn't seem to make sense. So why not continue the walk over the watershed, and take the route down another fine valley, Dentdale, to Sedbergh? But even Sedbergh - in those days still part of the old West Riding of Yorkshire - didn't make sense. Better it seemed to take it that little bit further along the River Lune to the old West Riding county boundary at Crook o' Lune Bridge in the Lune Gorge. From there it seemed logical to continue into what was still Westmorland, and across the foothills of the Lake District National Park to Bowness on the shores of Lake Windermere itself.

And so the idea of the Dales Way was born. The concept was the brainchild of two people – the late Tom Wilcock, boilermaker and trade union leader from Bradford, and

Walkers climb up from Lowgill on the 40th anniversary walk organised by the Dales Way Association in 2009

honorary footpath secretary of the West Riding Ramblers, and Colin Speakman of Leeds, English teacher at a local grammar school and area access secretary.

Following a pioneering walk along most of the route by Bradford Grammar School Venture Scouts in 1969, Fleur and Colin Speakman completed the first full detailed survey of the Way in Spring 1969. In summer 1969, the first public walk on the Dales Way between Ilkley and Bolton Abbey took place, 120 people turning up for the event which had been featured in the local press.

Colin Speakman & Tom Wilcock

The Countryside Commission, which was responsible for new long-distance paths, was approached, but at that time was also pursuing a possible Pennine Way - Lake District link. The two authorities, Westmorland and West Riding county councils, though sympathetic, were, as always, short of funds, and indicated that creating the Dales Way was not a priority.

So the Ramblers decided to take matters into their own hands and promote the route using existing rights of way covering 90% of the proposed Way, arguing that people, not bureaucrats, created paths. Within a year, the first guidebooks appeared in local bookshops and the Ramblers were promoting the route in newsletters and in the local press. More walks were arranged; soon an important new section of path was negotiated by Tom Wilcock near Farfield Hall, Addingham, to avoid a busy stretch of the B6160.

Local government reorganisation in 1974 slowed down progress as there were new bodies to deal with, but by then walkers had taken the Dales Way to their heart, its popularity increasing year by year.

More guidebooks were written and in 1991 the Dales Way Association was established to care for and promote the Dales Way with a view to it becoming a national trail. The association soon had over 400 members, nearly a fifth of whom were accommodation providers along the route. In the late 1980s the Countryside Agency actually shortlisted the Dales Way for national trail status, but a lukewarm response from the Yorkshire Dales National Park at that time held back development.

Ironically it was the terrible foot and mouth epidemic of 2001/2 that changed all that. Deprived of walkers, the tourist economy of the Yorkshire Dales suffered cataclysmic losses and when in 2002 the footpaths were re-opened, walkers were welcomed back. The attitude of the National Park Authority changed overnight, and the Dales Way was seen as a superb example of truly sustainable tourism with Dales Way walkers, especially those who stay overnight, making a major contribution to the local economy.

Since that time, there has been close collaboration between the Dales Way Association and national park field staff in constantly developing and improving the route, culminating in a 40th anniversary walk in 2009 over the whole route, which was launched by the Duke of Devonshire who cut a special Dales Way birthday cake at Bolton Abbey.

The People's Path had truly come of age.

(Opposite) Drawing of the route by E. Jeffrey from the original 1970 edition.

LAKE DISTRICT

Windermere

Bowness

R. Kent

To Penrith

Kendal

M6

To Lancaster

R. Lune

Sedbergh

R. Dee

Dent

Carlisle

Settle

R. Ribble

PENNINE WAY

Key

‒ ‒ ‒
ROUTE ALREADY DEFINITIVE
FOOTPATH _____

+ + +
PROPOSED ROUTE ~ FOOTPATH
REQUIRED _____

• • • •
SUGGESTED TEMPORARY
ALTERNATIVES _____

∘∘∘∘
PROPOSED DALES WAY
EXTENSIONS _____

‒ • ‒ • ‒
NATIONAL PARK
BOUNDARIES _____

Buckden

Kettlewell

Grassington

R. Nidd

BOLTON PRIORY

Harrogate

Ilkley
Otley

Bradford

R. Wharfe

The
DALES WAY
81 MILES
ILKLEY to BOWNESS

Leeds

Strid Woods (above left). The Strid in winter (above right).
St Peter's Church, Addingham (below).

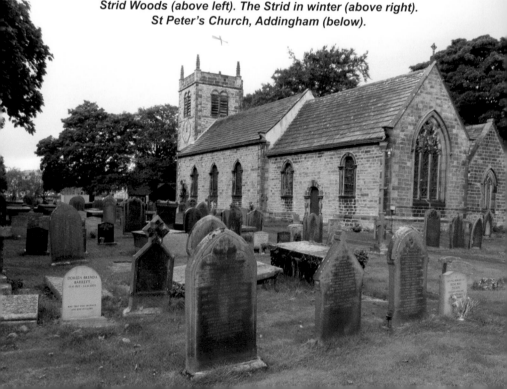

The little town of **ILKLEY** on the River Wharfe has a history as long as any in Yorkshire. There was undoubtedly a settlement here on the shallow ford across the Wharfe in Iron Age times, which must previously have been in regular use by the Neolithic and Bronze Age farmers who left their intriguing cup and ring markings on rocks all over the adjacent moors. When the Romans finally conquered the warlike Celtic Brigante tribes, some writers suggest that the old Celtic village name of Llecan was romanised to Olicana. For some centuries a small fort guarded the ford where Roman campaigning roads crossed the river en route from Elslack to the west, or Boroughbridge or York in the east. Remains of the walls of the Roman fort can still be seen behind the parish church and Tudor Manor House.

The Anglian and later Viking invaders also found Ilkley very much to their liking, and anglicised the name to something close to modern Ilkley (*ley* being a common Saxon suffix for a farmstead, a word gradually extended to mean a settlement).

For centuries the town remained a sleepy backwater, unlike Skipton or Otley without a market charter, and was largely missed by the industrial revolution. But things did change in the 18th century when the local squire, alerted to the alleged healing properties of the ice cold waters of the moorland springs, built the tiny Bath House, which still survives as White Wells, a landmark on Ilkley Moor passed by both the Leeds and Bradford Dales Way links. But it was the coming of the turnpike roads in the mid 18th century and the Midland Railway in the 1860s that accelerated Ilkley's growth into the "Heather Spa" noted for its healing waters and the clear, fresh air as an antidote to the new but polluted industrial towns of northern England. It soon became a popular commuter town, most especially for generations of wealthy

Old Bridge, start of the Dales Way

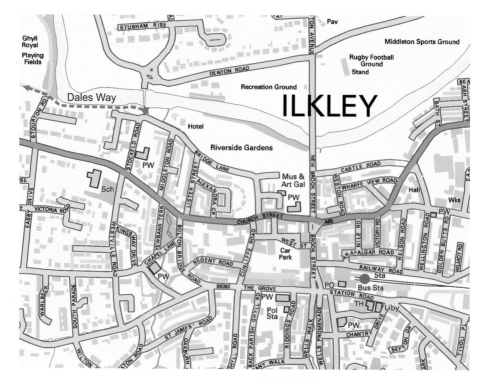

Bradford wool merchants and manufacturers, who built their fine villas mainly to the west of the town.

Ilkley remains a popular place both to live and to visit, with its elegant shops, riverside park and walks and above all Ilkley Moor, that magnificent stretch of heather moor and rough grassland rising up to 400 metres above sea level. It is a precious area of common land, celebrated worldwide in folk song, owned by the people of Ilkley and Bradford, where the public have enjoyed a legal right to walk freely for generations, a right that is still cherished.

How appropriate therefore that Ilkley became one of Britain's first Walkers are Welcome towns, with shops, cafes, inns and bed and breakfast establishments making a special effort to welcome walkers, and to ensure that walking routes out of the town are well looked after, none more so than the Dales Way.

These Anglo-Saxon crosses are now kept inside Ilkley's All Saints Church

18

Stage One: 9½ miles (15 km)

ILKLEY TO BARDEN

It's difficult to imagine a better starting point for a long-distance walk than Ilkley. Situated on the very edge of the West Yorkshire conurbation, with excellent public transport, including frequent electric train services from Leeds and Bradford and regular buses, it's also exactly where the true Dales country begins.

1 The official start of the Dales Way is the recently erected stone bench which lies close to historic Ilkley Bridge. Ilkley Bridge is not the relatively modern cast iron single span Middleton Bridge at the bottom of New Brook Street which carries road traffic over the river, but the far older 17th century hump backed bridge reached by walking a further 250 metres upstream through the riverside park. Until Middleton Bridge was built in the late 19th century, this was the only bridge crossing of the Wharfe between Otley and Bolton Bridge near Bolton Abbey.

The first section of the Dales Way is obvious and easy, and semi-urban. You follow the riverside track upstream behind houses and gardens, soon joining the narrow (but sometimes busy) road leading to the Ilkley Tennis Club and Sports Centre.

As you reach the Sports Centre and parked cars, look for the metal gate on the left, signed Dales Way, which leads to a path heading across fields through more small gates. Keep ahead as the path narrows over a footbridge going behind a riverside pump house, climbing a slope before once

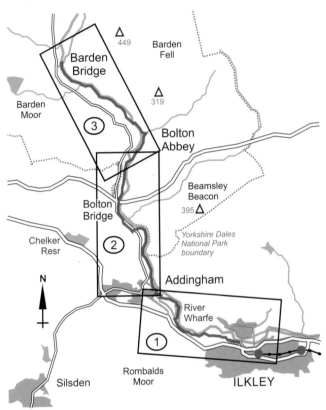

again returning to the riverside through a long narrow field below woods. Sections of path can be boggy here, so care is sometimes needed.

The path emerges on the old road to Addingham, part of the old Otley-Skipton turnpike road, now mercifully bypassed, and with a pavement alongside the river. Turn right at the first junction, along Old Lane to Low Mill village, past the large residential development which has taken over the Low Mill. Keep ahead into Low Mill

19

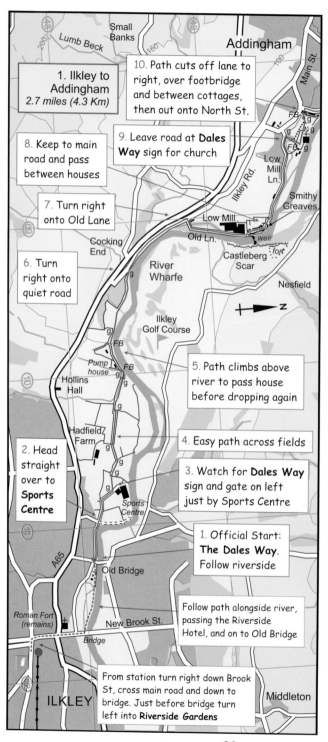

Small Banks

Lumb Beck

Addingham

Main St.

1. Ilkley to Addingham
2.7 miles (4.3 Km)

10. Path cuts off lane to right, over footbridge and between cottages, then out onto North St.

FB

8. Keep to main road and pass between houses

9. Leave road at Dales Way sign for church

Low Mill Ln.

Ilkley Rd.

Smithy Greaves

7. Turn right onto Old Lane

Low Mill

Old Ln.

weir

Cocking End

Castleberg Scar

fort

6. Turn right onto quiet road

River Wharfe

Nesfield

N

Ilkley Golf Course

FB

Pump house

FB

Hollins Hall

5. Path climbs above river to pass house before dropping again

Hadfield Farm

4. Easy path across fields

2. Head straight over to Sports Centre

Sports Centre

3. Watch for Dales Way sign and gate on left just by Sports Centre

A65

Old Bridge

1. Official Start: The Dales Way. Follow riverside

Follow path alongside river, passing the Riverside Hotel, and on to Old Bridge

Roman Fort (remains)

New Brook St.

Bridge

i

From station turn right down Brook St, cross main road and down to bridge. Just before bridge turn left into Riverside Gardens

Middleton

ILKLEY

village – a former mill workers' hamlet whose little terraced homes and former industrial buildings have been transformed into very desirable residential cottages.

Go through the gap stile at the end of the lane, keeping ahead on Low Mill Lane, past more cottages and fine houses. As you approach Addingham church, look for the pedestrian gate on the right which leads down steps to a stone humpbacked pedestrian bridge. Head for the church ahead, through the stile into the churchyard before turning left in front of the handsome church to join the main tarmac path to the churchyard entrance.

St Peter's, Addingham's parish church, with its magnificent blue clock, dates mainly back to the 15th century. It almost certainly replaced a far older church which in turn replaced an Anglo-Saxon preaching cross of the 9th century. Legend has it that in 872 AD the Anglo-Saxon Bishop Wulfhere of York fled here to escape attacks on York by marauding Danes before eventually finding sanctuary with King Burgred of Mercia.

Follow the main path through the gate and over a small footbridge which leads into North Street. Unless you are heading for the cafés, pubs, public toilets or bus stops in Addingham, turn right here.

2 Keep ahead for 100 metres past the layby and the village interpretation boards where the road curves left, to a gap on the right leading to steps down to the suspension bridge. Don't cross, but take the path along the riverside, an attractive section which emerges at High Mill, another former woollen mill converted to residential apartments. Head past the former mill through the gate and into the caravan park, looking for the waymark that directs walkers back to the riverside embankment.

The Dales Way now enters open countryside, a lovely section of riverside path, soon climbing a short bank above a cliff close to Farfield House where a stile on the right leads to a short flight of steps back down to the river. Continue to where river and path curve to the main B6160 road by a house garden. Cross with extreme care, but

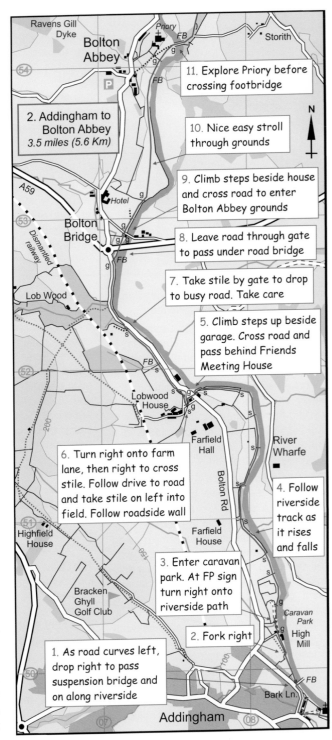

Ravens Gill Dyke

Bolton Abbey

Priory FB

Storith

g

g

P

FB

11. Explore Priory before crossing footbridge

N

2. Addingham to Bolton Abbey
3.5 miles (5.6 Km)

10. Nice easy stroll through grounds

9. Climb steps beside house and cross road to enter Bolton Abbey grounds

A59

Hotel

Bolton Bridge

g

g g

FB

g

8. Leave road through gate to pass under road bridge

7. Take stile by gate to drop to busy road. Take care

Lob Wood

s

5. Climb steps up beside garage. Cross road and pass behind Friends Meeting House

FB s

Lobwood House

s g s

g s

s

Dismantled railway

Farfield Hall

s

River Wharfe

6. Turn right onto farm lane, then right to cross stile. Follow drive to road and take stile on left into field. Follow roadside wall

Bolton Rd

s

4. Follow riverside track as it rises and falls

Highfield House

Farfield House

s

3. Enter caravan park. At FP sign turn right onto riverside path

s

s

Bracken Ghyll Golf Club

g

Caravan Park

2. Fork right

g

High Mill

1. As road curves left, drop right to pass suspension bridge and on along riverside

FB

Bark Ln.

Addingham

21

Addingham, or Long Addingham as it was known, was a busy manufacturing village, weaving both cotton and later wool. Buildings still survive in the village that contain 18th century weaving lofts which began to be linked together, to evolve into the world's first wool *manufactories* or mills. It is said that Addingham has more listed buildings than any other village in the Dales. The first water-powered mill in Addingham was developed by John Cunliffe (ancestor of the famous Bradford Cunliffe-Lister textile family) in 1789. The mill produced the very first piece of worsted yarn to be sold on Bradford market, and was probably the first successful worsted wool mill in the world. It was also the target of Luddite riots when in 1826 handloom weavers from Lancashire attempted to smash the new powered looms which they saw as a threat to their livelihood.

take the little gate straight ahead leading to and behind Farfield Meeting House.

This is the first of several sites associated with the early Quaker movement on or close to the Dales Way, and dates back to 1689. An interpretive plaque explains the history. The meeting house is open to the public on certain dates, but it is worth walking through the simple graveyard and peering through the windows to have a glimpse of the austerity and moving simplicity of the building.

From the gate behind the meeting house, turn right into the farm track, then right again over a stile to join a new driveway parallel to but away from the horrendously busy B6160. Where this rejoins the road go over a stile, continuing alongside the wall, still parallel to the road, to a stile by a gate where the path rejoins the road. Cross with great care, picking up the very narrow pavement on the far side. Go down the hill, passing a highway gravel storage area used as a badly sited car park, and through a pedestrian gate to steps and a footbridge. Take the riverside path under the roaring A59 to a cottage just below the twin stone arches of the old Bolton Bridge, bypassed by the A59 and now only carrying a byway.

Cross the road (not the bridge) to enter a lovely section of path, by steps and gates, directly opposite. This follows the riverside, crosses pasture then back to the riverside as the River Wharfe sweeps around a broad curve to Bolton Priory. Keep ahead over a small footbridge to join the broad and usually very busy gravel path below the priory. Turn left up the hillside to the steps and the gateway through the old priory wall to the village of Bolton Abbey – a perfect place to enjoy refreshment (tea shop in the village, refreshment kiosk and toilets by post office). There should be adequate time to visit the church and accompanying priory ruins, and to experience and enjoy a very special part of the Yorkshire Dales.

The Dales Way continues over the wooden footbridge below the priory, which runs parallel to the stepping stones known as Friars' Steps. Turn left from the bridge but bear right up the steps and along the high level woodland path which offers fine views back over the priory. Where the path reaches Hazlewood Lane, descend to the ford, using the footbridge over Pickles Gill to the right, returning towards the riverside and through the gate on the right to the riverside path to reach and eventually cross the wooden bridge at Cavendish Pavillion – another welcome all year refreshment stop for walkers, with toilets.

The Dales Way follows the main track through Strid Woods, though you can, if you choose, take one of a choice of waymarked loop trails through the woods (nature trail guide available from the shop at the entrance to the woods). These are all permissive paths through Strid Woods, a richly fascinating local nature reserve, noted for birdlife, wildflowers and lichens. Keep on the riverside to the awesome Strid itself.

This is where the entire River Wharfe passes through a narrow gritstone gorge scarcely two metres wide, hence the Strid or Stride. However it is also extremely deceptive as here the river has gouged out deep underwater canyons. Please heed all warning notices and keep children and any dogs under firm control. Many lives have been lost here, even in very recent times,

The Boy of Egremond

According to legend, the most famous victim of the Strid was the Boy of Egremond. He was the son of Alizia de Romille, lady of Skipton Castle in the twelfth century, and heir to the Romille family fortunes. The Romilles were Norman baronial landowners of Skipton Castle and other vast areas of northern England. Their name survives in Rombalds Moor, the great watershed between Wharfedale and Airedale of which Ilkley Moor forms just a part. It seems the boy was out walking with his favourite greyhound on a leash when he made his fatal leap across the Strid. The greyhound drew back at the last moment and the unfortunate youth was sucked under the raging torrent. The most moving part of the story, as related in an old ballad, concerns the forester who found the boy. The man, hardly daring to tell his mistress Alizia the dreadful tidings on his return to the castle, simply asked her, "What is good for a bootless bene?" meaning what can help when even prayer is useless. The lady, instantly realising the tragedy, simply replied, "Endless sorrow." It is said that in her grief she gave the land at Bolton to the Augustinian canons who were already recently established at nearby Embsay, to allow them to move to this much more attractive site. Sceptics have pointed out that this is unlikely to have been the case as Alizia's son was himself a signatory to the priory's initial charter for the land at Bolton; the historian Whitaker suggested that the Boy of Egremond might have actually been the son of William Meschines and Cecilia de Romille, Alizia's parents (Alizia kept her mother's name) and therefore actually her brother. But the story provided inspiration for Wordsworth's poem *The Force of Prayer* and for a rather less well known version *The Boy of Egremond* by Samuel Rogers (1763-1855), a once celebrated, but now largely forgotten minor poet. Custom has it that a ghostly white horse appears close to the Strid shortly before another death.

The Strid is seen at its best when the river is not too high, when the many whirlpool-carved rocks are exposed alongside the narrow chasm containing the river. This is a very special landscape. The paths through these woods were originally laid out in the early years of the 19th century by a very remarkable character, the Reverend William Carr, who, as well as being vicar of Bolton Abbey, was a literary and dialect scholar (he met Wordsworth) and amateur landscape architect. Carr laid out many of the walkways and cleared trees to offer suitable romantic vistas and views across and along the river, making Strid Woods one of the most fascinating early 19th century picturesque landscapes in Britain.

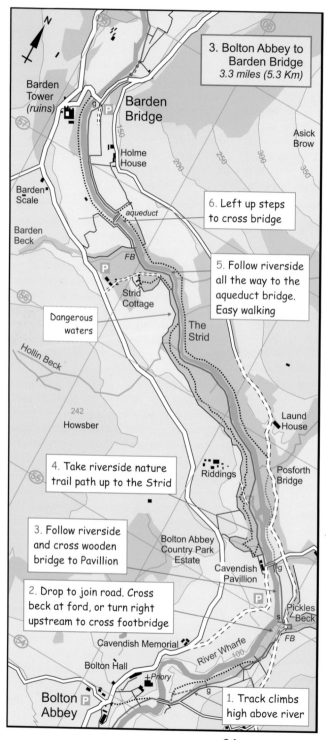

3. Bolton Abbey to Barden Bridge
3.3 miles (5.3 Km)

Barden Tower (ruins)

Barden Bridge

Asick Brow

Holme House

Barden Scale

Barden Beck

aqueduct

6. Left up steps to cross bridge

FB

5. Follow riverside all the way to the aqueduct bridge. Easy walking

Strid Cottage

Dangerous waters

The Strid

Hollin Beck

242
Howsber

Laund House

4. Take riverside nature trail path up to the Strid

Riddings

Posforth Bridge

3. Follow riverside and cross wooden bridge to Pavillion

Bolton Abbey Country Park Estate

Cavendish Pavillion

2. Drop to join road. Cross beck at ford, or turn right upstream to cross footbridge

Pickles Beck

Cavendish Memorial

River Wharfe

FB

Bolton Hall

Priory

Bolton Abbey

1. Track climbs high above river

attempting to leap across the gap, which is difficult to judge. Victims are trapped by the force of the powerful current and once in the water, face almost certain death.

Continue along the footpath which climbs to the left, sharply up the hillside through woods. At a fork, paths left go up to the Strid café, toilets and bus stop, but the Dales Way takes the right fork to descend to the riverside.

Cross another small footbridge and through a gate to where the Dales Way follows a much calmer stretch of riverside, soon reaching the crenellated Barden Aqueduct carrying water from the former Bradford Corporation Upper Nidderdale reservoirs towards Bradford. Take the steps on the left leading up to and over the aqueduct, returning to the riverside to pass fields and a large open expanse of grass where cars park in summer, to reach the beautiful 17th century stone arched Barden Bridge.

If you are ending your day's walk here turn left over the narrow bridge, to head up to the main road and bus stop outside the ruined tower.

24

Bolton Priory

Bolton Priory

(Bolton Abbey is the name of the village) dates from 1154 when Augustinian canons moved here from a site in nearby Embsay. The Augustinian or Black canons were slightly different from most orders of monks in that they took vows of obedience and chastity but not of poverty. Priory account books record prodigious amounts of food and drink being consumed on occasions. Fine clothes and good hunting were also enjoyed by successive priors and canons.

The priory suffered heavy loss of life and of possessions in 1318 when Black Douglas and his Scots invaders, driven south by starvation following extensive crop failures, raided Craven. The last prior, Richard Moon, sent Thomas Cromwell a gift of ten pounds in order to put off the inevitable dissolution in 1538. This did not impress Cromwell, and Richard's fine half built west tower remained unfinished until it was finally roofed by parishioners of the surviving Priory Church (now Bolton Abbey's fine parish church) in the 1970s.

The ruins, in a perfect riverside setting, together with later Tudor and 17th century buildings such as the old medieval gatehouse converted into a shooting lodge, are extremely beautiful, and have attracted poets, painters, guidebook writers and photographers for generations, including such figures as Turner, Landseer and Ruskin.

This landscape has been looked after by successive generations of the Clifford, Burlington and Cavendish families, later the Dukes of Devonshire, who have always welcomed visitors. The estate is now managed by the trustees of the Chatsworth Estate, who continue to care for this magnificent Dales landscape and natural heritage with its riverside, woods and surrounding heather moorland of Barden Moor and Barden Fell to which visitors have had access for half a century. This welcome has also included Dales Way walkers since the route's inception in 1969. Walkers in turn have respected the estate's very special qualities and recognise the contribution made by the estate to both landscape and footpath conservation.

Bolton Priory even has a ghost – a moving tale recorded with due pathetic colouring by William Wordsworth after he had been staying at New Grange, Kirkstall in 1807 and had travelled by horse and carriage to Bolton. In the autumn of that year he had read Whitaker's *History of Craven* and was moved to write his *White Doe of Rylstone*, considered in the 19th century to be one of his most perfect creations.

It concerns the Norton family, of Rylstone at the far side of Barden Moor, who as Catholics supported the ill-fated Rising of the North of 1569 and died at the scaffold for their folly. Legend has it that Francis Norton was buried in the churchyard at Bolton Priory. He – like Wordsworth – had a very close relationship with his sister, known as Emily. He gave her a little white doe that he had trapped, as a token of his affection. After Francis's death and the ruin of the family, Emily continued to make her melancholy journey over the fell to visit her brother's grave, accompanied by the white doe. It is said that after her death the white doe was still seen by country folk on the Sabbath and looked like a "gliding ghost". Pathos in verse is unfashionable but Wordsworth's poem remains very moving.

And there must be some truth in the story, because the ancient bridleway climbing high over Barden Moor between Rylstone and Bolton Abbey still exists and is now a popular route for both walkers and cyclists. It passes the ruined summerhouse owned by the Norton family known as Norton Tower, and can still be seen, though the Norton's old manor house at Rylstone is now nothing more than a few uneven mounds in a field.

Barden Tower dates back to the 15th century when it was a former keeper's lodge in the old hunting forest of Barden, a former huge deer park extending as far as Skipton. It was owned by the Clifford family, for four centuries lords of Craven and Skipton. During the Wars of the Roses, the notorious "Butcher" Clifford – so called because of his cruel murder of the young Duke of York - was himself killed when the Lancastrians defeated the Yorkists in the terrible battle of Towton in 1461, and his wife, Lady Margaret, feared for the life of her own children.

Her eldest son Henry was, according to legend, given to a family of shepherds to bring up as their own son in Cumberland – though it may well have been the Yorkshire Wolds where the Cliffords also had land. But when Henry Tudor took the throne after the Battle of Bosworth in 1485, Henry successfully petitioned the new King Henry VII, and his lands in Craven and title were restored as he became the tenth Lord Clifford. Though he had no formal education, he was taught to read and write by the canons of Bolton Priory, preferring to live at Barden, to enjoy "the silence that is the starry sky" rather than the noisier surroundings of Skipton Castle, in the simple lodge he rebuilt into a modest-sized fortified house. A good and wise man, known and respected as the Shepherd Lord, he fought for his king against the Scots at the battle of Flodden in 1513, despite being almost 60 years old.

Until a few years ago, a local farmer and his mother ran the nearby Priest's House (now a restaurant) as a tea shop, and halberds that once belonged to the Shepherd Lord's men and used at Flodden were displayed in the tea room. The Shepherd Lord's son, also called Henry, enjoyed a somewhat wild and dissolute youth as a companion of the wild Prince Hal who was later to become King Henry VIII (his story recorded in a remarkable anonymous ballad called The Nut Brown Maid). In his mature years, like the king a reformed character, he was made Duke of Cumberland, a title which was to survive several centuries.

In the 17th century, the last of the great Clifford family, the energetic and charismatic Lady Anne Clifford, who is still remembered for her philanthropy in both Yorkshire and Cumbria, restored the tower where her mother had lain "greate with child". A stone plaque on the wall of the tower placed there by Lady Anne herself recalls the event.

The Dales Way crosses some of the finest countryside the Yorkshire Dales National Park has to offer:

Dentdale (above); Upper Wharfedale near Hubberholme (left); River Wharfe near Burnsall (below).

Opposite: Farm near Lincolns Inn Bridge (top); Leaving Outershaw heading for Cam Fell (bottom).

The Yorkshire Dales National Park

The Dales Way offers the walker a perfect introduction to the Yorkshire Dales National Park. Established in 1954, but extended in 2016 the Yorkshire Dales is now England's second largest national park, covering 871 square miles of breathtakingly beautiful scenery across England's central Pennines. It stretches from Bolton Abbey and the outskirts of Skipton and Settle to the south; to the Orton Fells and watersheds of the Swale, Ure and Eden in the north; from the Howgills and Lune valley in the west; and to the edge of what is now the Nidderdale Area of Outstanding Natural Beauty east of Wharfedale and Coverdale.

The gritstone crags and drier heather moorlands in the eastern part of the national park contrast with the spectacular limestone scenery of cave and crag to the west, rising in the south-west to the highest summits of the Three Peaks – Pen-y-ghent (694 metres), Ingleborough (724 metres) and Whernside (736 metres), all to be seen in their dramatic setting from the Dales Way in its central stages.

The southern part of the national park is also crossed by the impressive fault lines of the three great Craven Faults, where huge dislocation of the earth's crust has resulted in many of the great limestone cliffs and crags of the western Dales, such as Attermire Scar, Malham Cove and Gordale Scar. But by the time the South and Mid Craven Faults extend to cross the Wharfe at Loup Scar and Linton Falls on the Dales Way, the dislocation is relatively minor and the landscape features, whilst still impressive, are on a smaller scale.

But it is the deep valleys, the Dales themselves, carved out from the bedrock by the abrasive action of glaciers and fast flowing rivers over countless millennia, that give the Dales their special character, added to by numerous side valleys or gills where waterfalls cascade down the steep v–shaped vale sides. The character of the Dales comes from the contrast between fertile valleys and bleak, open-topped hills or fells – their barrenness resulting from human activity over the last ten thousand years, felling trees and grazing animals, or in many areas cultivating heather for sporting activity.

The Dales are also notable for complex patterns of stone barns and walls – countless miles of dry stone walls, erected to enclose small and larger pastures from medieval times onwards, but especially in the 18th and 19th centuries when many of the ancient common lands were enclosed to achieve agricultural efficiency. Traditional forms of livestock farming have shaped this landscape in other ways. Scattered farmhouses, often on the sites of monastic granges, and dating from the 17th century, are a characteristic feature of every Dale, together with small copses and shelter belts of woodland. Of special importance are the maintenance of the traditional Dales meadows whose rich, lush flower- and herb-rich hay crop was harvested and stored in the thousands of small stone Dales barns, with their haylofts and cattle byres, which now are such a distinctive and special feature of the Dales landscape.

In Britain, a national park is not nationally owned nor is it a park. It is an area where a combination of strict planning laws, government grants and environmental schemes protect that special landscape. Thanks to good visitor management, for example of footpaths, car parks and public access areas, as well as high quality information and education services,

Limestone pavement above Conistone

visitors are able to enjoy the area without damaging its special qualities. The national park authority is a democratically elected body (with a minority of members appointed to represent the national interest) employing a small specialist staff. Their challenge is to balance the needs of the local community with those of visitors; visitors for whom the national park offers wonderful opportunities for outdoor pursuits which enhance physical and mental well-being, and who in return contribute so much to the local economy. At the same time the national park must protect and conserve an area of national and even international importance, noted for its biological diversity, its archaeological richness, its industrial and cultural heritage and its scenic splendour. Looking after the Dales Way is just one way of achieving such a balance.

BARDEN TO GRASSINGTON

For most people the seven fairly gentle miles between Barden Tower and Grassington village isn't a full day's walk. You could simply give yourself an easy day with time to explore Grassington, or extend the first and third stages to Burnsall, perhaps making use of the local bus service that parallels the Dales Way, to and from a convenient overnight accommodation base. There is limited parking near Barden Bridge but buses stop on request outside the main entrance to Barden Tower.

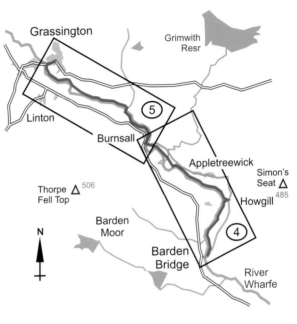

Whatever you choose, take time to discover Barden Tower. If you are walking up from Barden Bridge, half way up the road look for a stile on the left which gives pedestrian access through the old lodge gateway to this impressive if ruined medieval hunting lodge.

4 From Barden Tower a path leads from behind the right hand side of the tower through the little stone archway and down to a stile in the lane. Turn right (take care with traffic), down to Barden Bridge, a lovely 17th century stone humpbacked bridge in a beautiful setting.

The Dales Way continues from the far side of the usually busy layby car park, where a narrow path has recently been constructed between wall side and river to keep walkers away from the busy road. This leads uphill to a gate directly ahead which takes walkers back along the main riverside path.

The next mile is easy walking, between field and river, through a number of small gates to where the path narrows between willows and fence. This section, popular with angler and mallard, eventually passes the stepping stones at Drebley and bears right past the farmyard at Howgill, joining the lane by Howgill Bridge at a small crossroads.

Turn left here over the bridge, then left again over a stile to follow an especially attractive stretch of the Dales Way below Haugh Wood, soon alongside river and woods, with dramatic white water rapids beloved of canoeists. Beyond the rapids, gate and small footbridge, the path enters a longer field, makes its way over a little hummock and below a popular caravan and camp site.

A narrow walled green lane, known as

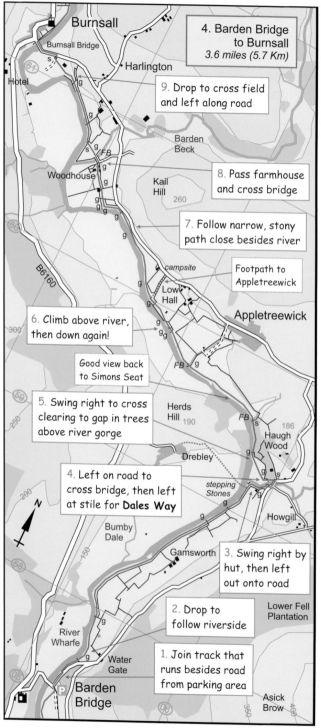

Onion Lane (because onion sellers once sold their wares there, perhaps as part of Appletreewick Fair), gives access to the village. Otherwise keep along the riverside, as the path once again narrows alongside rapids.

This is where on the Dales Way the character of the landscape changes. After walking so far through countryside dominated by that harsh form of rough, dark Pennine sandstone known as millstone grit, the lighter-coloured, smoother carboniferous limestone is much more in evidence. This section of the Way actually squeezes along the edge of Kail Hill – one of the famous Lower Carboniferous Craven reef knolls, formed 250 to 300 million years ago as the accretions of billions of skeletons and shells of tiny sea creatures formed huge circular reefs under the tepid waters of a great lagoon. Limestone produces sweeter soils and therefore you will see more wild flowers - campions, cowslips, rockroses, violets, primroses, orchids, as you walk northwards.

Burnsall Bridge in winter (above).

River Wharfe near Howgill in autumn (above and left). Appletreewick in the distance, with Simons Seat to the right (below).

The village of **Appletreewick** (locally pronounced Ap'trick), little more than a hamlet with some fascinating Tudor houses, is just visible across the fields. The village still has two pubs, perhaps a reminder that in 1311 the village was granted a charter for a long-forgotten fair on the 27th and 28th October of each year where cattle, sheep and ponies were sold. Appletreewick was also the birthplace of a wealthy London merchant, Sir William Craven, who went to London a penniless apprentice, but by 1611 had become lord mayor. Many people claim he was the source of the folk tale of Dick Whittington and his cat.

This section of Dales Way can flood when the river is exceptionally high, and even on drier days you squeeze your way over and between tree roots and stones, eventually turning right to cross a couple of fields and through the yard of Woodhouse Farm. Keep ahead across the main farm entrance to the footbridge and a narrow enclosed way which climbs another hillock before swinging round to the large open field – used as a riverside car park and picnic area in the summer months. Keep ahead to the edge of Burnsall Bridge. Turn left over the bridge to the village.

Burnsall was once a Viking settlement, as two amazing hog-back gravestone covers in the little church testify; the village name is a corruption of *Bjorn's Hall*. It is in a perfect setting, in a great arc of the river between the heather-covered fells, with a riverside village green complete with maypole, its 17th century grammar school (still the local primary school) endowed by Sir William Craven, a street of 18th and 19th century cottages and houses, and a handsome church and old inn. Burnsall is an inevitable tourist magnet.

5 The Dales Way continues from Burnsall Bridge below and to the right of the Red Lion. This popular section of riverside path has been transformed into a full wheelchair accessible stretch to allow everyone to enjoy a magnificent stretch of the Dales Way which runs opposite Loup Scar – an impressive limestone escarpment.

Loup Scar also has its macabre side. In 1766 the body of a local physician, Dr Petty, was discovered here. He was murdered by Grassington inn keeper and local blacksmith Tom Lee, in order to silence him after the doctor had witnessed a robbery. Lee was duly caught, tried and hanged at York Tyburn and his decaying corpse swung for some years from a gibbet at Donkey Hill, by Grassington Bridge, to discourage other villains. The tale inspired several Victorian balladeers and penny novelists, and a plaque on a small building – now an art shop – in Grassington's main street indicates it was once Tom Lee's old smithy.

Beyond the accessible walk, the Dales Way climbs over a steep knoll, with fine river views back across the Scar, enters a short stretch of woodland and passes more pleasant riverside to reach Hebden Swing Bridge. This steel and wire footbridge, which can rock unnervingly on a windy day, was originally built at the end of the 19th century by the Hebden blacksmith, but was totally reconstructed in recent years. After crossing the bridge you now follow a much calmer, quieter section of deep, slow moving river by an avenue of chestnut trees, giving a feeling of parkland to this section of riverside, with only the occasional gate or stile and a small

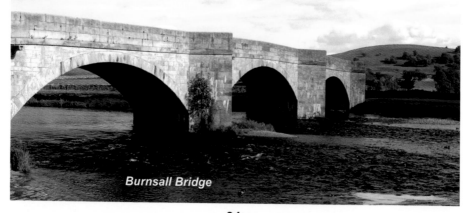

Burnsall Bridge

footbridge to slow progress. The path goes through scattered woodland below Lythe House, then across an open field past the water treatment works. Across the river, the low towerless church ahead is Linton Church, sometimes called the cathedral of the Dales.

Linton Church dates back to the 12th century. It has only a small bell tower and is Norman in layout (though much restored in the 19th century). It probably occupies the site of an old Anglo-Saxon preaching cross. Stepping stones lead across the river direct to the church, but the Dales Way goes though the gate on the right, and along an access road. The tall house on the left is a former mill, on the site of Grassington's ancient water-powered manorial corn mill. The trout farm on the right, fed by a powerful underground stream which bursts to the surface at this point, is on the site of a lead smelt mill, the spring water which drains from Grassington Moor powering the waterwheels and machinery.

Follow Mill Lane uphill for 250 metres to where a step stile on the left gives access to a path which crosses two fields down to Linton Falls.

This is an area of fierce rapids and waterfalls caused by the Mid Craven Fault, a geological shifting of the underlying limestone strata which crosses the River Wharfe at this point, producing the dramatic waterfalls. The iron pedestrian bridge gives a superb vantage point over the falls. Dippers are usually active in the rills and pools of the river. Historically the falls and the massive weir above have played an important role in the history of Grassington. Up to the 1980s there was a textile mill with a huge mill chimney here, initially a water-powered corn mill, later spinning cotton, wool worsted and in its latter stages man-made fabrics. Waterwheels initially provided power, in later years replaced by a water-powered turbine and a fine steam engine, which is now in Bradford Industrial Museum. The mill was demolished and replaced by housing in the early 1980s, but the mill owner's house remains. The line of old cottages where once the mill workers lived close by was known as Botany, perhaps because to live there away from the villages of Linton or Grassington was like being exiled to Australia's Botany Bay.

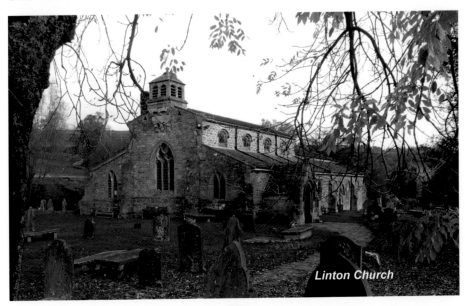

Linton Church

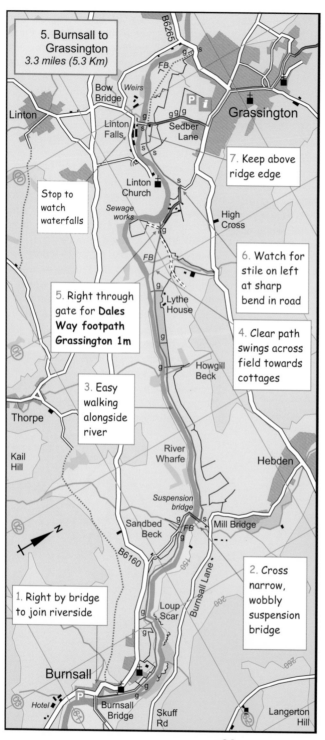

5. Burnsall to Grassington
3.3 miles (5.3 Km)

Bow Bridge
Weirs

Linton

Linton Falls

Sedber Lane

Grassington

Linton Church

7. Keep above ridge edge

Stop to watch waterfalls

Sewage works

High Cross

6. Watch for stile on left at sharp bend in road

FB

5. Right through gate for Dales Way footpath Grassington 1m

Lythe House

4. Clear path swings across field towards cottages

Howgill Beck

3. Easy walking alongside river

Thorpe

Kail Hill

River Wharfe

Hebden

Suspension bridge

Sandbed Beck

FB

Mill Bridge

2. Cross narrow, wobbly suspension bridge

B6160

1. Right by bridge to join riverside

Loup Scar

Burnsall Lane

Burnsall

Hotel

P

Burnsall Bridge

Skuff Rd

Langerton Hill

The second higher weir upstream provided power for a very early hydro-electric scheme which until the 1950s gave Grassington village its electricity. It was not always reliable at times of drought or heavy frost and boiling a kettle could take some time. Ironically history has repeated itself as the new Grassington Hydro twin Archimedes screw generator provides power not only for the people of Grassington but feeds into the National Grid.

Turn right up the narrow, enclosed gravel path, known locally as *Snakey*, which leads up to the National Park Centre, car park, toilets, picnic area and grandly titled Transport Interchange with local buses back to Barden, Bolton Abbey and Ilkley, down to Skipton or up the dale to Buckden.

Most people choose to end a stage of the Dales Way here – either staying in a choice of guesthouse accommodation or taking advantage of good transport links on a day walk. The village has a choice of cafes, pubs, good shops, including outdoor shops and a guaranteed warm welcome for Dales Way walkers.

Below Loup Scar (top).
Garrs Lane, Grassington (left).
Conistone Pie (above).

Grassington, a village occupying shallow limestone terraces above the steep valley sides of the River Wharfe, has an immense history. Almost certainly the original Iron Age and Romano–British village settlement was on higher land, on terraces above the village known as Lea Green where foundations of ancient hut circles and small enclosures can still be deciphered in late afternoon sunshine or under light snow. The village moved lower down the slopes in Anglo-Saxon times, doubtless to capture the natural water supplies of emerging springs; an ancient pump in the village square is a relic of this communal water supply. It grew to become the main township in Upper Wharfedale and in 1282 it was granted a charter for a fair and market. The market has long vanished but the ghost of the fair lingers on in the annual children's Sports or Feast held every autumn.

Grassington

But it was in late medieval times, and even more so in the 17th and 18th century, that the village, or township as it should be called, grew in size and importance because of rich mineral wealth to be won from nearby hills: lead. In the boom years of the 18th and 19th century, miners working on Grassington Moor were housed in hovel-like houses built around tiny courts or folds around the Square. Their little free time was catered for by several public houses, three of which survive, their spiritual improvement by three non-conformist churches and a fine mechanics institute – now the Devonshire Institute and town hall.

The decline of lead mining led to depopulation of the village which was only reversed by the coming of visitors, first by train on the long vanished Skipton-Grassington Yorkshire Dales Railway (opened in 1902), then by massive increases in road transport, first charabancs and buses, then private cars in the 20th century. Some of the miners' cottages have survived into the 21st century as bijou weekend or retirement homes, restaurants, souvenir shops or speciality boutiques. The village now hosts the nationally renowned Grassington Festival of Music and Arts each June whilst December weekends are crowded with coach and car loads of visitors seeking the somewhat ersatz Dickensian Grassington experience – Charles Dickens never came anywhere near the village.

Stage Three: 10½ miles (17 km)

GRASSINGTON TO BUCKDEN

The section of the Dales Way through Upper Wharfedale is deservedly one of the most popular sections of the whole route because of magnificent panoramic views as you make your way across classic karst limestone country. Ironically, the 6½ miles between Grassington and Kettlewell were originally thought of as a temporary diversion loop, pending the day when linear access to the riverside between Grass Wood, Conistone and Kettlewell could be negotiated. Those negotiations never took place because of opposition from anglers and landowners, but most walkers now agree the diversion is even better than the proposed riverside walk.

6 Starting, no doubt after refreshment, from Grassington Square, head up Main Street, by the Devonshire Hotel, up to the town hall, turning left into Chapel Street. After 300 metres take the second narrow lane on the right, Bank Lane, (with Dales Way signs) which soon becomes a track. You have a choice here. After another 200 metres, a gate on the left takes the Dales Way over a little footbridge; it then heads across the field to two narrow stiles before turning right up a field and through more stiles to another narrow stile, leading to a path which rejoins the same track from Bank Lane. Alternatively (and much easier especially with a pack), is to continue through the gate up Bank Lane, a stony track which is not currently shown on the definitive map but has been used by walkers for at least 40 years.

This track bears left to where it is joined by the line of the official Dales Way, and then swings right, becoming a lovely grassy path ascending through Lea Green, an area of rich archaeological interest. Keep to the main path, slightly right, at a fork.

Look out on both sides of the path for a line of low hillocks and depressions which marks the line of ancient bell pits, probably medieval, along a lead vein. The wood on the left is Bastow Wood, which joins Grass Wood. This whole area is a wonderful nature reserve, again full of archaeological interest and locally celebrated for its rich and diverse flora, including the hauntingly beautiful bird's eye primrose, now the logo of the Yorkshire

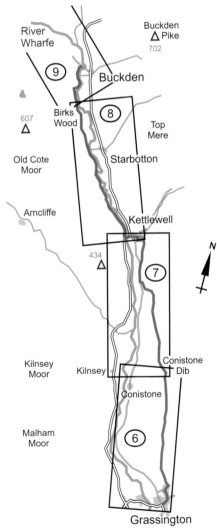

39

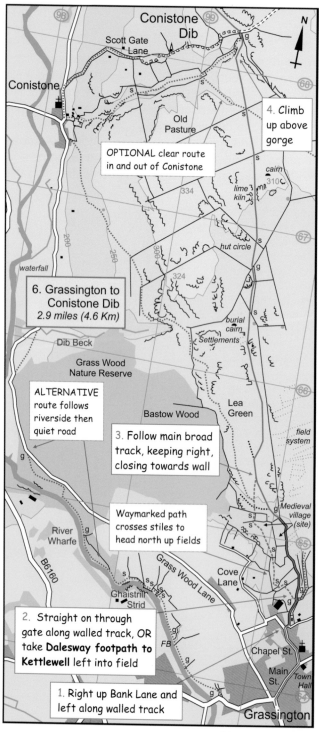

Conistone Dib

Scott Gate Lane

Conistone

Old Pasture

OPTIONAL clear route in and out of Conistone

4. Climb up above gorge

cairn

lime kiln

334

310

hut circle

waterfall

324

6. Grassington to Conistone Dib
2.9 miles (4.6 Km)

burial cairn

Dib Beck

Settlements

Grass Wood Nature Reserve

ALTERNATIVE route follows riverside then quiet road

Bastow Wood

Lea Green

field system

3. Follow main broad track, keeping right, closing towards wall

Waymarked path crosses stiles to head north up fields

River Wharfe

Medieval village (site)

Grass Wood Lane

Cove Lane

Ghaistrill Strid

2. Straight on through gate along walled track, OR take **Dalesway footpath to Kettlewell** left into field

FB

Chapel St.

Main St.

Town Hall

1. Right up Bank Lane and left along walled track

Grassington

Dales Society. Keep straight ahead, with the stone wall about 100 metres to your right. As you approach some impressive limestone scars, in layers, look for a ladder stile. Another faint mound to your left is the remains of a burial cairn. Other ancient earthworks are visible. Cross to the next gate and stile, the Dales Way clear on the ground ascending a steep slope to reach a fine, partially restored lime kiln.

Until the late 19th century, when lime was mass-produced in huge, mechanised quarries, small lime kilns like these, fired by wood or local coal, were used to turn crushed limestone rock into quicklime. These were "slaked" (by adding water) for use as mortar, to sweeten acid soil or as limewash to colour the inside or outside walls of buildings.

The Dales Way now follows a high, level terraced path, clearly marked over a series of often quite steep stiles and little gates. This was possibly a prehistoric terrace path used by early farmers and traders crossing between Wharfedale and Wensleydale.

Looking up Wharfedale to Kilnsey Crag

Though smaller than Grassington, **Kettlewell** is also a lead mining village which has survived and prospered into the age of mass tourism. Lead miners' cottages are also weekend retreats, but there are larger houses with some guesthouse accommodation, an outdoor shop, cafes and pubs as well as a post office, general store and youth hostel. The village car park is a favourite starting point of many fine walks: along the Dales Way to Buckden, Starbotton or back to Grassington; up Great Whernside; or across Old Cote Moor to Arncliffe and Littondale. There are toilets, and also the bus service back to Grassington, Ilkley and Skipton, or onward to Buckden.

Lead Mining in Upper Wharfedale

The discovery of great pigs of lead marked with Roman lettering in the Nidderdale area confirmed that lead has been mined there at least since Roman times, and the area has rich veins of galena or lead ore. Galena and barites (another valuable ore) are found in vertical veins close to the fault lines and fractures in the earth's crust where layers of carboniferous limestone and gritstone, under intense pressure, buckle, fracture and fold.

Earliest attempts to extract the ore were by simple primitive bell pits or day-holes dug along the vein, with side passages dug out and propped by timbers to extract the ore. Lines of bell pits can still be traced across surrounding moors above Grassington – one such is passed on the Dales Way. By the 17th and 18th century, mining techniques had improved, with professional mining engineers from the Harz mountains and Thüringen in Germany bringing deep mining techniques to Cornwall, Derbyshire and finally the Yorkshire Dales. Between the 17th and 19th century, successive dukes of Devonshire and their agents developed ever more sophisticated techniques to mine and smelt (refine) vast quantities of lead ore from the surrounding mines. A highly complex network of artificial reservoirs and water courses was built on Grassington Moor to capture water from moorland springs and tarns. This was then used to drive waterwheels to power machinery, pump water out of deep mineshafts and haul ore to the surface. A huge mill chimney and extended flue survives on the crest of Grassington Moor, together with storing, crushing, and dressing areas. The duke even built an underwater canal to drain the deepest shafts into nearby Hebden Gill (there were even plans to use the canal to carry ore in barges) and in the 1770s a new road was built from Grassington to Gargrave to access the new Leeds-Liverpool canal for onward shipment. It is said that lead from Grassington Moor not only helped to build but also to finance Chatsworth House in Derbyshire.

Main areas for lead mining activity in the Yorkshire Dales were Upper Wharfedale, Nidderdale, parts of Wensleydale and most of Swaledale - the most intensively mined dale of all.

By the 1880s, after periods of boom and bust, the industry finally collapsed owing to dwindling veins and cheap, mainly Spanish, imports carried by new cargo steamers and railways. Within a decade the industry had collapsed for all but a handful of miners, resulting in unemployment, extreme poverty and mass migration of families from the Dales to the rapidly growing industrial cities of Lancashire, West Riding and County Durham and even overseas, especially the USA and Canada.

Over a century of weathering and natural growth has now grassed over and renatured these vast areas of workings, buildings and spoil tips, though many areas, poisoned by centuries of pollution and industrial despoliation, remain desolate. But they tell a powerful story of man's struggle against the elements, of remarkable technical innovation in the early years of the industrial revolution, and also individual poverty and suffering, in the struggle to win a living in a harsh environment – the lifespan of most lead miners was pathetically short. Most of the ruins are now protected monuments, and those on Grassington Moor are interpreted by a mining trail. However many dangerous shafts remain half open and concealed, so do not stray off clear paths when walking in any former lead mining area.

Chimney & flue (1849), part of the lead mining system at Yarnbury above Grassington

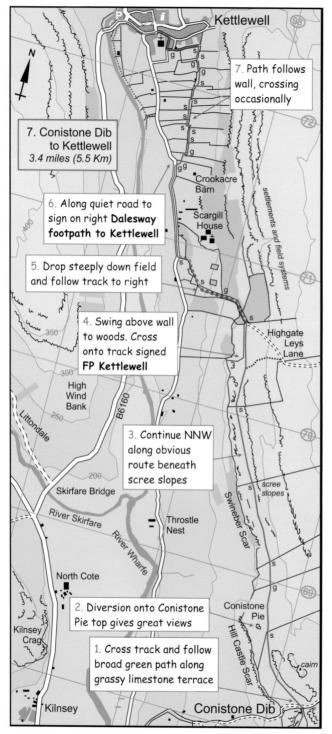

Kettlewell

7. Conistone Dib to Kettlewell
3.4 miles (5.5 Km)

7. Path follows wall, crossing occasionally

Crookacre Barn

6. Along quiet road to sign on right **Dalesway footpath to Kettlewell**

Scargill House

5. Drop steeply down field and follow track to right

4. Swing above wall to woods. Cross onto track signed **FP Kettlewell**

Highgate Leys Lane

High Wind Bank

3. Continue NNW along obvious route beneath scree slopes

B6160

Littondale

Skirfare Bridge

scree slopes

Swineber Scar

River Skirfare

Throstle Nest

River Wharfe

North Cote

2. Diversion onto Conistone Pie top gives great views

Conistone Pie

Kilnsey Crag

1. Cross track and follow broad green path along grassy limestone terrace

Hill Castle Scar

cairn

Kilnsey

Conistone Dib

settlements and field systems

As you walk there are ever more magnificent views across and along the valley to Kilnsey Crag and northwards up Wharfedale to Old Cote Moor and into the secluded valley of Littondale.

The Way eventually bears right and crosses above Dib Scar, a deep limestone gully, before ascending to reach a narrow track above a wireless mast.

This is Scott Gate, an old monastic track from Malham and Kilnsey used by the monks of Fountains Abbey. It is a continuation of Mastiles Lane which eventually crosses into Nidderdale.

From the crossroads, continue in the same direction. The Dales Way crosses open pasture below limestone scars, heading for a stile ahead.

The impressive limestone crag ahead is Conistone Pie, a fine viewpoint which appears to have been created by human hand, but was likely to have been formed by the action of one of the many glaciers that carved out the steep valley sides of Upper Wharfedale as well as the great lip of Kilnsey

7

Crag on the opposite side of the valley. On a clear day from this terraced path beyond Conistone Pie, you enjoy the twelve mile panorama, a magnificent expanse of Upper Wharfedale extending as far to the north as the crags at the head of the dale above Cray, and to the south to the finger-like war memorial tower on the summit ridge of Barden Moor high above Cracoe.

It is easy level walking along this beautiful limestone terrace above Swineber Scar but below other scars and scree slopes, high above the valley, the path marked by stiles and gates. You eventually reach a pine wood, and track on the left by a gate and stile. Go through here, following the stony track as it descends through more gates and stiles to reach the lane from Conistone.

As you descend there are intriguing views of Scargill House, notable for its remarkable Scandinavian style steep-roofed chapel, designed by York architect George Pace in 1960. Scargill House is a Church of England retreat and conference centre, a place of physical and spiritual refreshment, where Dales Way walkers are welcomed.

Follow the lane past Scargill for 400 metres until a gate on the right gives access to a field path. Follow the waymarks to the next gate and stile on the left. The Dales Way now follows the field wall over stiles, at first keeping the wall to your left and then to your right as you head towards the village of Kettlewell. As you approach the village, take the second track left, which goes in front of a cottage and through a gate to follow the Dales Way into Kettlewell. Turn right by the church, then left into the lane leading to the main road and bridge over Dowber Gill Beck by the Racehorses Inn.

8 North of Kettlewell the Dales Way returns to the riverside. From the village centre, walk along the main B6160 towards Skipton. Cross the main bridge over the Wharfe and turn sharp right to head for the gate by the edge of the bridge past the National Trust

sign. Fifteen metres beyond the gate, the Dales Way slopes down shallow steps to the riverside, joining a stony then concrete path by the river, curving past the confluence with Dowber Gill Beck, then turning upstream, through a gate on the right, then a series of gates and stiles – sometimes a combination of the two.

Path finding is easy along this well-trodden section, most walkers enjoying the popular circuit back to Kettlewell via Starbotton, the route clear through a sequence of gates and stiles, short stretches of enclosed path and a series of fields. Take care not to always follow broader tractor tracks but look for the narrower footpath through stiles.

The river meanders in a series of loops through the flat, glaciated valley bottom, now a flood plain of wet, reed-strewn pastures and pools, often flooded in the winter months. After periods of heavy rain or snowmelt the ancient glacial Upper Wharfedale lake can often re-appear.

The Way follows a slightly raised shallow shelf of well-compressed limestone scree and boulders, in some places on the outside of the field enclosures close to the river (a recent small diversion avoids a badly eroded section of embankment), through more fields to the footbridge leading across the river to Starbotton.

This footbridge has a dedication in memory of the late Harry Smith, a much-loved former chairman of the West Riding Ramblers whose friends contributed to the cost of its restoration.

Unless you are visiting Starbotton (its name literally meaning the small wood where poles or standards were cut) and the Fox & Hounds Inn, keep ahead along the riverside path across pasture. As the river curves away across the flood plain, the well-trodden way, clearly marked by gates and stiles, passes scattered barns, eventually becoming a partially surfaced green track enclosed between walls. It

Birks
Wood

Eshber
Wood

**8. Kettlewell to
Birks Wood**
3.3 miles (5.3 Km)

Walden Rd.

g
g
g

FB
s

Step Gill

s

ruin

**7. Keep to
wall as river
curves away**

N

Cam Gill Beck

River
Wharfe

s

Starbotton Cam Rd.

s

g
FB

Fosse
Wood

Starbotton

s
s

**6. Straight on
passing bridge**

Moor
End
Fell

s
FB
g

**5. Take gate on
right to drop
into wet pasture**

450

g

4. Keep right

FB
s
g
g

3. Swing to right

Cam
Pasture

**2. Easy path
to follow
above river**

400

Springs
Wood

g g

g

Paradise

Middlesmoor
Pasture

g

g

g

350

**1. Cross river bridge,
right through gate
and right again to
drop to riverside.
Dalesway footpath
Starbotton 2 ml**

300

250

Kettlewell

g

g

---

crosses a small footbridge before curving round to join a more elevated, broader track through parkland below Birks Wood .

A grove of giant redwood trees together with Austrian pines and other non-native species gives this part of the valley an incongruous, slightly exotic feel. These date from the 1850s when the then owner, Sir John William Ramsden, planted the woods to create a gentleman's country retreat. It is now part of the National Trust Upper Wharfedale Estate.

Follow the track for some 300 metres to where the Dales Way turns sharp right, signposted, descending to a pedestrian gate, twisting around an S-shaped loop, up to the flood bank alongside the river. Follow this bank, paved in places, past rustling willows and alders, to Buckden Bridge.

For Buckden, turn right across the bridge to follow the lane uphill, cutting across the village green to toilets, car park, village shop, cafés, pub and terminus of the Upper Wharfedale bus.

9

46

BUCKDEN TO GEARSTONES

This stage is perhaps the most strenuous day's walk on the Dales Way. Cam Fell at 520 metres (around 1,800 feet) is the highest point on the route, and though the climb from Langstrothdale is not steep, it is a long, slow ascent along tracks and across rough pastureland. It's easy enough in good weather conditions but if you are unlucky enough to have a strong westerly gale in your face and constant rain or sleet with no shelter or refreshment facilities for several miles, it can be tough going. Always carry ample food, protective clothing and water supplies with you, listen to weather forecasts and don't be afraid to turn back before Beckermonds if bad weather threatens.

Buckden with its reasonable accommodation base and good public transport links from Grassington, Skipton and Ilkley is an ideal starting point.

As its name implies, Buckden was originally a hunting lodge in the old Forest of Langstrothdale. Here *forest* denotes an ancient Norman and Plantagenet hunting reserve where game was protected and rigorous laws imposed, though some woodland (*dene* means woodland) remained as shelter for deer. In later centuries it became another Wharfedale village associated with lead mining; extensive old workings remain at Buckden Gavel on the side of the Pike.

Return to Buckden Bridge. A few metres beyond the bridge, a gate on the right leads to a lovely section of riverside path, continuing along raised embankments alongside the Wharfe which, north of Buckden, diminishes in size to little more than a broad stream.

Follow the path along the flood bank, through gates, until it bears sharp left to join the lane to Hubberholme. The National Trust and national park rangers are planning to make this path wheelchair accessible. Turn right in the lane, taking care with traffic, to reach the hamlet of Hubberholme.

The Dales Way continues over the bridge and along the track through the gate to the right of the church, soon bearing off left along a narrow path which goes above and behind the church along a steep hillside. This section of the Dales Way is extremely unstable, and the path

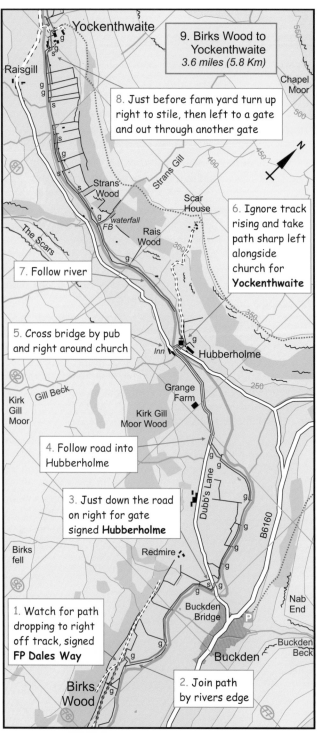

Yockenthwaite

9. Birks Wood to Yockenthwaite
3.6 miles (5.8 Km)

Raisgill

Chapel Moor

8. Just before farm yard turn up right to stile, then left to a gate and out through another gate

Strans Wood

Strans Gill

Scar House

6. Ignore track rising and take path sharp left alongside church for Yockenthwaite

waterfall
FB

Rais Wood

The Scars

7. Follow river

5. Cross bridge by pub and right around church

Inn

Hubberholme

Kirk Gill Beck

Grange Farm

Kirk Gill Moor

Kirk Gill Moor Wood

4. Follow road into Hubberholme

Dubb's Lane

3. Just down the road on right for gate signed Hubberholme

B6160

Birks fell

Redmire

1. Watch for path dropping to right off track, signed FP Dales Way

Buckden Bridge

Nab End

P

Buckden Beck

Buckden

Birks Wood

2. Join path by rivers edge

is frequently closed and diverted. The original path is however highly scenic, winding its way along the hillside with fine views across treetops to the far side of what is now a much narrower valley. Beyond the steep hillside the path returns to the riverside below first Rais Wood and then, after a little footbridge, Strans Wood. You follow a mile or so of classic Dales Way, past some wonderful herb-rich traditional hay meadows and riverside verges which in spring are brilliant with wild flowers – cranesbill, speedwell, sorrel, yellow rattle, rockrose and orchids. The path is marked by small gates or stiles, some of them quite narrow, but is easy to follow through a series of fields. As you approach the hamlet of Yockenthwaite, the path veers to the right through stiles and between the farm buildings, cottages and the fine Georgian farmhouse of Yockenthwaite itself. Head slightly uphill across the farm drive to where a finger post indicates the continuation of the Dales Way ahead through a small gate.

48

10 Another very attractive section of the Dales Way follows, edging between riverside and meadows. You pass a small lime kiln. Follow the green track by the riverside to a stile. Just by the wall further on is a little stone circle or henge monument, probably Bronze Age in origin, suggesting this part of the Dales Way has been in use for a very long time. A series of small gates takes you up to Deepdale Farm, where the Dales Way goes below the farmhouse to a small footbridge, keeping ahead through another gate to the road and bridge across the River Wharfe.

Cross, but take the track on the right on the far side of the river. This is a popular stretch of the Dales Way, the river now little more than a mountain stream sparkling and shimmering between rocks, a popular picnic place on warm days in summer as motorists park their cars on the verge to enjoy the open riverside – a great place for children to paddle.

Keep ahead past New House Farm, the track narrowing and rising above the river, eventually curving, over a stile, up to gates and a

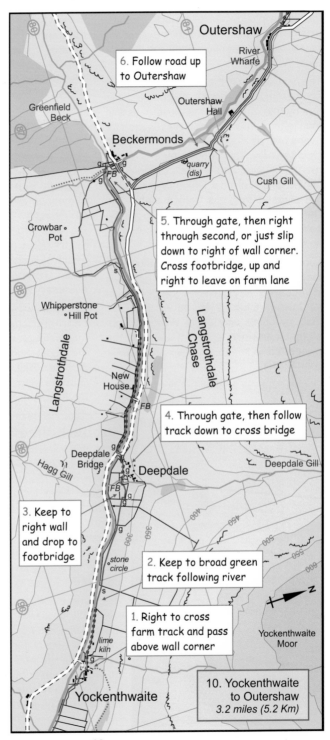

6. Follow road up to Outershaw

Outershaw

River Wharfe

Outershaw Hall

Greenfield Beck

Beckermonds

quarry (dis)

Cush Gill

5. Through gate, then right through second, or just slip down to right of wall corner. Cross footbridge, up and right to leave on farm lane

Crowbar Pot

Whipperstone Hill Pot

Langstrothdale

Langstrothdale Chase

New House

FB

4. Through gate, then follow track down to cross bridge

Deepdale Bridge

Hagg Gill

Deepdale

Deepdale Gill

FB

3. Keep to right wall and drop to footbridge

stone circle

2. Keep to broad green track following river

1. Right to cross farm track and pass above wall corner

Yockenthwaite Moor

lime kiln

Yockenthwaite

10. Yockenthwaite to Outershaw
3.2 miles (5.2 Km)

footbridge into the hamlet of Beckermonds, a name that literally means *the mouth of the becks*, where Greenfield Beck and the little River Wharfe meet.

The next section of the Dales Way is a bit of an anticlimax, as there is no choice but to turn right to go back to the crossroads and then left to follow the main Hawes road for over a mile as it ascends Low Bank over to Oughtershaw. This is not a busy or a fast road, but weekend traffic can make it unpleasant and most Dales Way walkers are pleased to get it behind them. The Dales Way Association has tried to get the path diverted to avoid the tarmac but so far no solution has been found.

Look out however for the very attractive former school and chapel on the right, built in Venetian style in polished granite by local landowner Charles Wood in 1856, in memory of his wife Lydia Wilson Wood, almost certainly to the design of the celebrated Victorian art critic and painter John Ruskin.

Oughtershaw is a small but pretty hamlet,

the last habitation in Langstrothdale before the tarmac road ascends Fleet Moss towards Hawes. The Dales Way keeps straight ahead past the stone Celtic cross erected to commemorate Queen Victoria's golden jubilee in 1887. Take the left fork here, along the gated track, a gentle climb up to Nethergill Farm, continuing beyond towards Swarthgill ahead.

Beyond Swarthgill the Dales Way crosses rough pastureland, alongside walls, through gates, crossing several tiny streams or sikes, each feeding down into Oughtershaw Beck, the principal source of the River Wharfe. From here the river flows for 61 miles (about 97 kilometres) to its mouth at its confluence with the River Ouse near Cawood, south of York, and eventually to the Humber.

In clear weather, as you climb, the characteristic flat-topped summit of Ingleborough will soon come into view. To the south and east, Fountains Fell and Buckden Pike will be in evidence, together with the long, almost treeless valley you have climbed out of, Langstrothdale.

Hubberholme, which retains its Norse name, has a fine old church, dating from medieval times. It is one of the few churches in England to retain a Tudor rood loft, a high balcony in front of the altar. Most were torn down by Cromwell's puritans in the civil war, but thankfully the zealots do not appear to have penetrated as far as Langstrothdale. The great Yorkshire writer and broadcaster J.B.Priestley (1894-1984) declared Hubberholme his favourite place and his ashes are scattered close by.

The nearby George Inn, established here in medieval times to provide refreshment for churchgoers, retains the curious custom of a New Year's Eve auction for the renting of the Poor Field in the hamlet. When a candle lit for the purpose by the local parson burns out, the highest bid for the annual grazing rights to the field is accepted and the rental income used to help the poor of the parish.

The Upper Wharfedale Estate

As the Dale curves westwards, it takes the name Langstrothdale – literally the dale of the long valley, *stroth* or *strath* being a corruption of the Gaelic word *srath*, meaning broad valley, a name dating from the Irish-Viking invasions of this part of the Dales.

This part of Langstrothdale and much of Upper Wharfedale now form part of the National Trust's magnificent Upper Wharfedale Estate, the bulk of which was given to the National Trust by Graham Watson, former managing director of Manningham Mills in Bradford. Graham, a passionate conservationist, who served on both the Lake District and Yorkshire Dales National Park committees, and who was a founder member of the Yorkshire Dales Society, used part of his considerable wealth from Bradford's textile industry to purchase land in Upper Wharfedale. In 1989 Graham gave his 2,000 hectare estate, in the heart of the national park, including much of Buckden Pike, to the National Trust - for ever, for everyone - in memory of his brother David who had recently passed away.

Cam Fell High Road has a long history. Almost certainly it was one of the great military or campaigning roads constructed in the first century by Roman general and engineer Julius Agricola between his forts at Lancaster and Bainbridge in Wensleydale. It remained in use as the main route for both coaches and carriers' waggons carrying people and goods from the old port of Lancaster on the west coast to Wensleydale, Richmond and north-east England for many centuries. By the 18th century, wheeled traffic had increased so much that in 1751 it was rebuilt and improved for the newer, faster stagecoaches as part of the new Lancaster-Richmond turnpike. The cost of the improvement was financed by a turnpike trust, wealthy local merchants and landowners who recouped their investment from tolls paid by road users. It became a key trans-Pennine highway, serving Askrigg where new inns were built to feed tired travellers and provide fresh horses for coaches.

However in 1795 the entire route of the turnpike between Ribblehead and Wensleydale was rebuilt to take advantage of much gentler gradients via Newby Head and Widdale, reducing the immense effort required by horses which had to haul heavy coaches or

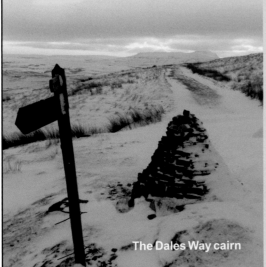

The Dales Way cairn

waggons over murderously steep gradients. This new road made Hawes, rather than Askrigg, the principal coaching town of Upper Wensleydale. The old road over Cam Fell remained in use as bridleway and footpath but vehicle rights still exist. Damage by four-wheel drive enthusiasts resulted in welcome traffic regulation orders, which have helped to conserve this most important and beautiful green highway which now carries both the Pennine Way and Dales Way long-distance footpaths. However, planning approval in 2013 means that Cam High Road is now used by 44 tonne waggons transporting timber out of Cam Forest.

51

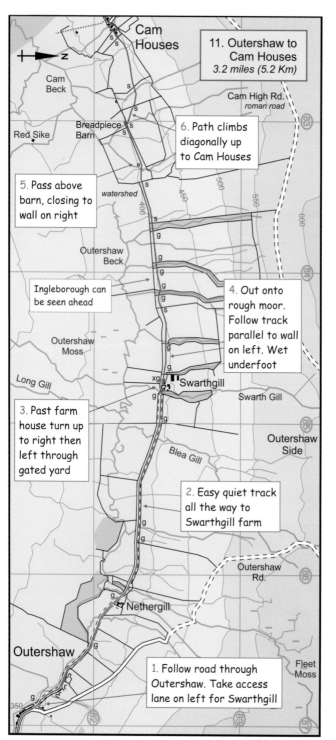

Cam Houses

Cam Beck

Red Sike

Breadpiece Barn

5. Pass above barn, closing to wall on right

watershed

Outershaw Beck

Ingleborough can be seen ahead

Outershaw Moss

Long Gill

3. Past farm house turn up to right then left through gated yard

Cam High Rd.
roman road

6. Path climbs diagonally up to Cam Houses

500
450
400
550
660

g
g
g
g
g
g
g
xg
g
g

Swarthgill

Swarth Gill

Blea Gill

2. Easy quiet track all the way to Swarthgill farm

g
g

Outershaw Side

Outershaw Rd.

g

Nethergill

Outershaw
g

350
g

1. Follow road through Outershaw. Take access lane on left for Swarthgill

Fleet Moss

11. Outershaw to Cam Houses
3.2 miles (5.2 Km)

4. Out onto rough moor. Follow track parallel to wall on left. Wet underfoot

---

A steady ascent now, through a bleak landscape. Keep alongside walls and pass above a barn, heading to Breadpiece Barn, above which the path climbs moorland to a group of buildings at Cam Houses, one of the wildest and remotest farms in the Yorkshire Dales. The farmhouse is now a holiday cottage and no longer caters for Dales Way walkers.

Take a little care at the farm (see map). Do not follow the main farm drive, but make your way behind the buildings and left through a gate and stile to head across the next small field towards Cam Woodlands, a coniferous plantation. Waymarks will guide you through the end of the plantation to a steep hillside where you need to climb diagonally up the field to a stile in the fence above.

There is an alternative route here: if you are heading for Dentdale you can choose to shorten the Dales Way by around a mile and a half by turning right from Cam Houses to take the path up over access land, curving past Gayle Moor End and Cam Cob to join the Ribble Way and new Pennine Bridleway, descending

12

52

Gayle Moor to Newby Head and the Dent Road (see pg. 55 - the watershed alternative).

Keep ahead in the same direction until you finally join the Cam High Road at the Dales Way cairn – at 520 metres above sea level the summit of the Dales Way.

If you are lucky enough to have a fine day for this section, the views as you walk will be unforgettable: to the west, the magnificent profiles of all the Three Peaks - Ingleborough, Whernside and Pen-y-Ghent - will appear before you, offering an overwhelming sense of space and light.

Easy walking now, with ever changing views, as the Dales Way takes the long descent along the Cam High Road, soon passing another cairn at Cam End where the Pennine Way diverges towards Ling Gill and Ribblesdale. Fine views of the famous Ribblehead viaduct on the Settle-Carlisle line can be enjoyed from here. The Dales Way descends quite steeply past Round Hill down to the broad ford and bridge across Gayle Beck - a principal source of the River Ribble.

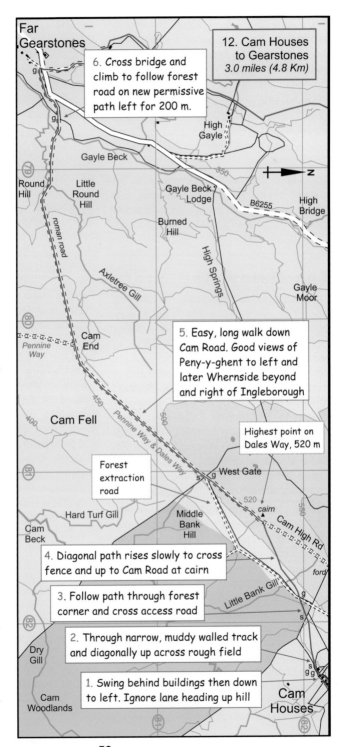

Far Gearstones

6. Cross bridge and climb to follow forest road on new permissive path left for 200 m.

12. Cam Houses to Gearstones
3.0 miles (4.8 Km)

High Gayle

Gayle Beck

Round Hill

Little Round Hill

Gayle Beck Lodge

B6255

High Bridge

roman road

Burned Hill

High Springs

Axletree Gill

Gayle Moor

Cam End

Pennine Way

5. Easy, long walk down Cam Road. Good views of Peny-y-ghent to left and later Whernside beyond and right of Ingleborough

Cam Fell

Pennine Way & Dales Way

Highest point on Dales Way, 520 m

Forest extraction road

West Gate

cairn

Cam High Rd

Hard Turf Gill

Cam Beck

Middle Bank Hill

520

ford

4. Diagonal path rises slowly to cross fence and up to Cam Road at cairn

3. Follow path through forest corner and cross access road

Little Bank Gill

2. Through narrow, muddy walled track and diagonally up across rough field

Dry Gill

1. Swing behind buildings then down to left. Ignore lane heading up hill

Cam Woodlands

Cam Houses

53

The Ribble heads for Preston, the Ribble estuary and Irish Sea rather than Hull and the North Sea, the final destination of the waters of the Wharfe. You have crossed the watershed of England.

From the bridge follow the track up to the gate. Turn left along the busy B6235 for 200 metres to where the next stage of the Dales Way starts below Holme Hill north of Gearstones.

The old house at Gearstones, now an outdoor centre and bunkhouse, was until 1911 an old drovers' inn where, before the coming of the railway in the 1870s, Scottish drovers spent the night as they brought their herds of cattle south to the cattle fair on Malham Moor. The cattle were fattened on the rich limestone pastures of Craven before travelling to the fair and then onward to feed the growing cities of the English Midlands.

You may well wish to walk for another mile and a half (2 km) down the road to Ribblehead Station to the welcoming Station Inn with food, local ale and overnight accommodation (B&B and bunkhouse) or take a train along the famous Settle-Carlisle line back to Skipton or Leeds.

The Dales Rail Story

Local stations on the Settle-Carlisle line closed in 1970. As a result of a very successful West Riding Ramblers excursion train in 1974, in the following May the Yorkshire Dales National Park committee agreed to charter special weekend trains which called at the then near-derelict stations at Horton–in–Ribblesdale, Ribblehead, Dent, Garsdale and Kirkby Stephen, along with connecting buses to Hawes and Sedbergh and a popular programme of guided walks. These were Britain's first ever trains for walkers chartered by a national park.

The pilot scheme proved a huge success, with several hundred people using the trains and buses, including local people who could also use the trains for shopping in Leeds, Skipton or Carlisle. The scheme was extended through the summer and autumn of 1975; the following year, additional stations in Cumbria were reopened, and special Lancashire Dales Rail trains operated from Manchester and Blackpool calling at Clitheroe. By the early 1980s Dales Rail services were operating once a fortnight throughout the summer months, and tens of thousands of people were taking advantage of the new network.

Despite plans to close the line because of claims that Ribblehead Viaduct was too expensive to repair, British Rail was encouraged to expand the weekend-only local trains to a daily service, ostensibly to take students to Carlisle. This increased usage dramatically. No doubt this was helped by the wide publicity the closure proposals had received. Legal opinion established that Dales Rail trains had indeed formally reopened the local stations. This meant many thousands of walkers could join the rail enthusiasts objecting to the closure. By the time the line was officially saved in 1989, it had become one of the region's top tourist attractions. But it is now also a major Anglo-Scottish freight artery, and millions of pounds of investment have secured the future of the line some have dubbed one of the world's most scenic railways.

It is certain that, had it not been for Dales Rail and the reopening of the local stations to serve the national park, especially Dent and Ribblehead which are so valuable for Dales Way walkers, the Settle-Carlisle line would now be no more than a memory or, at best, a crumbling, expensive-to-maintain cycle way.

Deepdale in Langstrothdale (top). Beckermonds (centre). Cam Houses (bottom).

Tom's Pennine Way and Mary's Pennine Bridleway

The Dales Way is crossed on Cam Fell by both Britain's oldest and newest national trails.

In the 1930s Tom Stephenson (1893-1987), journalist, rambler, access and national park campaigner, and the first full-time paid secretary of the Ramblers Association, had a vision of a long green trail between the Peak District and Scotland. It finally came to fruition in 1965 as Britain's first long-distance trail - the Pennine Way. This 251 mile (404 km) route from Edale in Derbyshire to Kirk Yetholme in Scotland shares a mile with the Dales Way along the Cam Fell High Road between the Dales Way cairn above Cam Forest and Cam End.

Tom Stephenson's vision undoubtedly inspired Lady Mary Towneley (1936-2001), wife of a former Lord Lieutenant of Lancashire, and a lifelong campaigner for bridleway rights, to develop the concept of an extended bridleway, using existing ancient green ways as well as new routes, between Derbyshire and Scotland. This was based on a long ride she had made in 1986 with three friends, travelling between Ashbourne in Derbyshire and Hawick in the Scottish Borders. Mary persuaded the Countryside Commission (later Natural England) to develop and fund the new 347 mile (558 km) route for horseriders, walkers and mountain bikers, to be known as the Pennine Bridleway. The route, which also goes through the heart of the Yorkshire Dales, is not yet fully open, but a superb new section of engineered bridleway between Selside and Garsdale came into use in 2012.

The Pennine Bridleway also meets the Dales Way at Cam Fell, and now offers a very fine alternative route into Dentdale via Cam West End and Gayle Moor, then along the Ribble Way past Newby Head, to Galloway Gate where it joins the Coal Road

above Dent Station.

This is a dramatic section of route in its own right, with an option of saving a mile and a half on the original Dales Way via Gearstones, so it could become a popular alternative, though Gearstones and Ribblehead offer perhaps more options than Denthead for refreshment, accommodation and transport at the end of a long day's hike from Buckden.

Stone House farm beneath Artengill Viaduct

The Dales High Way, a 90 mile hill walk between Saltaire in Airedale and Appleby in Cumbria, is the creation of publishers, walkers and writers Tony and Chris Grogan. Recognised as a long-distance path by the Long Distance Walkers' Association, the Dales High Way provides a fascinating high level parallel route, to the west of the Dales Way. The two routes intermingle in parts of Dentdale between Dent and Sedbergh before the Dales High Way heads off on a six-mile ridge walk across the Howgill Fell range, then through the little-known but beautiful limestone country of the Orton Fells to Appleby.

It's the perfect companion piece to the Dales Way, albeit more strenuous, which means that once having walked the Dales Way you might consider tackling the greater challenge of the Dales High Way. Details of Dales High Way maps and guide are at the end of this volume.

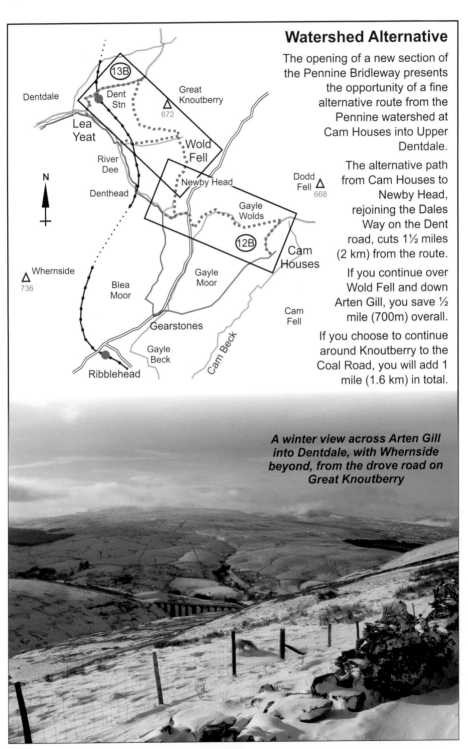

Watershed Alternative

The opening of a new section of the Pennine Bridleway presents the opportunity of a fine alternative route from the Pennine watershed at Cam Houses into Upper Dentdale.

The alternative path from Cam Houses to Newby Head, rejoining the Dales Way on the Dent road, cuts 1½ miles (2 km) from the route.

If you continue over Wold Fell and down Arten Gill, you save ½ mile (700m) overall.

If you choose to continue around Knoutberry to the Coal Road, you will add 1 mile (1.6 km) in total.

A winter view across Arten Gill into Dentdale, with Whernside beyond, from the drove road on Great Knoutberry

Map labels:
13B
Dentdale
Dent Stn
Great Knoutberry
△ 672
Lea Yeat
Wold Fell
River Dee
Newby Head
Dodd Fell △ 668
Denthead
Gayle Wolds
N
12B
Cam Houses
Whernside △ 736
Blea Moor
Gayle Moor
Cam Fell
Gearstones
Gayle Beck
Cam Beck
Ribblehead

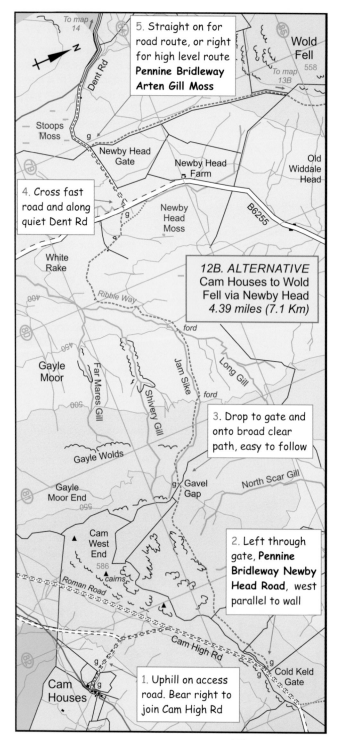

5. Straight on for road route, or right for high level route **Pennine Bridleway Arten Gill Moss**

Wold Fell

To map 14

Dent Rd

Stoops Moss

Newby Head Gate

Newby Head Farm

Old Widdale Head

To map 13B

4. Cross fast road and along quiet Dent Rd

Newby Head Moss

B6255

White Rake

Ribble Way

12B. ALTERNATIVE Cam Houses to Wold Fell via Newby Head **4.39 miles (7.1 Km)**

ford

Gayle Moor

Far Mares Gill

Jam Sike

Shivery Gill

Long Gill

ford

3. Drop to gate and onto broad clear path, easy to follow

Gayle Wolds

Gayle Moor End

Gavel Gap

North Scar Gill

Cam West End

586

cairns

Roman Road

2. Left through gate, **Pennine Bridleway Newby Head Road**, west parallel to wall

Cam High Rd

Cold Keld Gate

Cam Houses

1. Uphill on access road. Bear right to join Cam High Rd

From the back of Cam Houses, fork right and head steeply uphill along the farm access road. Bear right at a T-junction and continue up to join the Cam High Road. Turn right on here for 700 metres to reach Cold Keld Gate. Go through this and take the field gate on the left marked *Pennine Bridleway Newby Head Road*. Bear left, heading west parallel to the wall on your left along a clear grassy track, with excellent views down Snaizeholme Beck to the north.

Drop to a gate in the wall ahead at Gavel Gap and follow the clear broad path, now the Ribble Way, alongside Jam Sike and Long Gill down to the B6255 at Newby Head. Cross the road and continue along the quiet Dent Road for 400 metres to reach Newby Head Gate on your right.

You have a choice now: straight on along the road to rejoin the Dales Way which follows the road down into Dentdale; or right through the gate marked *Pennine Bridleway Arten Gill Moss* to climb steadily towards Wold Fell for a longer but stunning high level alternative.

12B

The clear path follows the wall on the right, up through a gate and into a short enclosed track. Through the next gate, the path continues ahead, not always clear on the ground, along the dip of a minor dry valley. Long views up Widdale to the north-east open out.

The path begins to descend, veering left to rejoin the wall, down to Arten Gill Moss at a gate on a broad green lane that crosses ahead. Go left through the gate.

There's a choice here: a shorter alternative is to follow the bridleway down beside Arten Gill to Stone House to rejoin the Dent road; or take the gate on the right marked *Pennine Bridleway Coal Road* which leads to a short climb before bearing left to follow the contour around Great Knoutberry, with long views down Dentdale and across into Garsdale to the north. This is part of the old drove road known as Galloway Gate.

Eventually at a T-junction you join the Coal Road, turning left to follow the road, as it descends quite steeply past Dent Station and down to Dent Road at Lea Yeat.

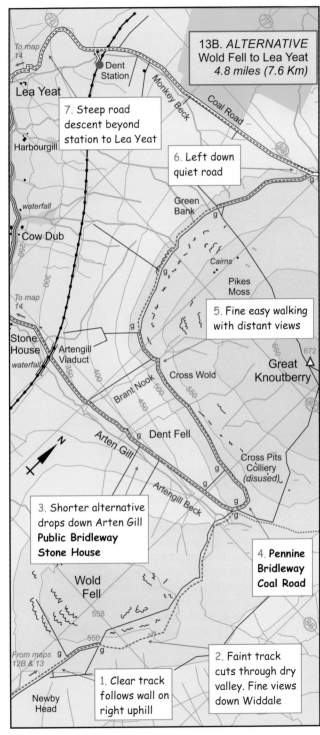

13B. *ALTERNATIVE*
Wold Fell to Lea Yeat
4.8 miles (7.6 Km)

To map 14

Dent Station

Lea Yeat

Monkey Beck

Coal Road

7. Steep road descent beyond station to Lea Yeat

Harbourgill

6. Left down quiet road

waterfall

Green Bank

Cow Dub

Cairns

Pikes Moss

To map 14

5. Fine easy walking with distant views

Stone House

Artengill Viaduct

waterfall

Great Knoutberry

Cross Wold

Brant Nook

Arten Gill

Dent Fell

Cross Pits Colliery (disused)

Artengill Beck

3. Shorter alternative drops down Arten Gill
Public Bridleway Stone House

4. **Pennine Bridleway Coal Road**

Wold Fell

558

550

From maps 12B & 13

2. Faint track cuts through dry valley. Fine views down Widdale

1. Clear track follows wall on right uphill

Newby Head

Stage Five: 14 miles (23 km)

GEARSTONES TO SEDBERGH

The Dales Way through Dentdale is one of the loveliest means of experiencing one of the truly magical Yorkshire Dales, where the landscape begins to show those subtle differences and changes as it enters Cumbria (though historically still part of the ancient West Riding of Yorkshire) and approaches the Lake District.

Unless you are breaking your journey at Dent, this is a long stage, a full 14 miles, and perhaps even 16 if you are staying at Ribblehead or walking from the railway station, and continuing into Sedbergh itself rather than Millthrop. However the going is relatively easy with some stretches of lane or track along which distances can be covered quickly and easily.

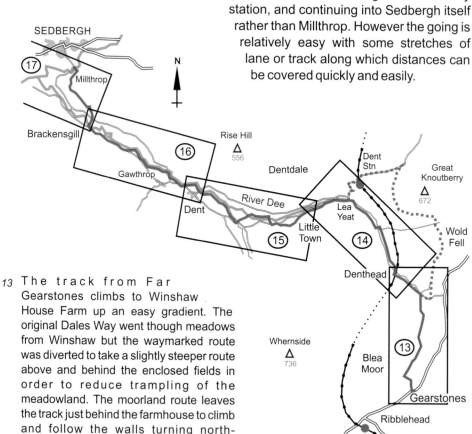

13 The track from Far Gearstones climbs to Winshaw House Farm up an easy gradient. The original Dales Way went though meadows from Winshaw but the waymarked route was diverted to take a slightly steeper route above and behind the enclosed fields in order to reduce trampling of the meadowland. The moorland route leaves the track just behind the farmhouse to climb and follow the walls turning north-westwards, through stiles and along the side of Gate Cote Hill, with good views back towards Ingleborough and Pen-y-Ghent.

Beyond High Gayle, the path joins Black Rake Road, a stony track coming in from the right. It then heads due north over the moorland of Stoops Moss and curves along the edge of a hillside to eventually reach the Newby Head - Dent road a short distance above Dent Head Viaduct, where you'll probably look down on a freight or passenger train on the Settle-Carlisle line below you.

14 A choice here. At present the Dales Way follows this road for just over 3 miles (5 km). But it is a beautiful country lane (though it can be busy in the summer season) leading under Dent Head Viaduct down into Upper Dentdale, one of the few dales, here at least, to run northwards. The valley bottom is shared by the little River Dee.

Look out for boulders and even pebbles of "black marble" here. Black Marble is limestone with high carbon content. This stone was much prized in Victorian times as, when carved and polished, the tiny fossils in the rock stood out in white, giving the rock a marble-like appearance. It was quarried locally and much prized for mantelpieces and fireplaces, or ornate columns in country mansions. The stone was even used in station buildings on the Settle-Carlisle railway.

Continue as far as Stone House.

To your right you see the massive Artengill Viaduct where an ancient track leads up Arten Gill to join a packhorse track which crosses the pass

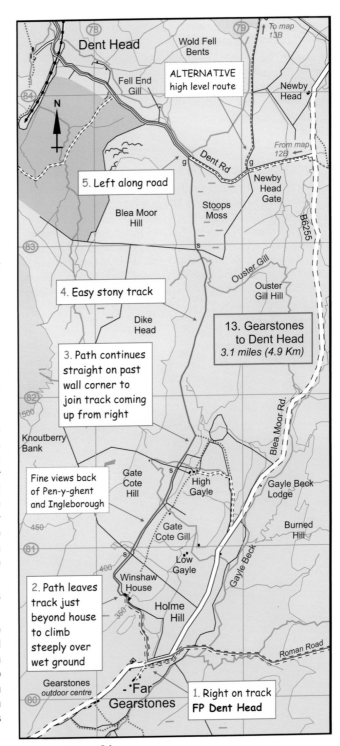

Dent Head

Wold Fell Bents

ALTERNATIVE high level route

Fell End Gill

Newby Head

N

Dent Rd

Newby Head Gate

5. Left along road

Stoops Moss

Blea Moor Hill

B6255

Ouster Gill

Ouster Gill Hill

4. Easy stony track

Dike Head

13. Gearstones to Dent Head
3.1 miles (4.9 Km)

3. Path continues straight on past wall corner to join track coming up from right

Blea Moor Rd.

Knoutberry Bank

Gate Cote Hill

High Gayle

Gayle Beck Lodge

Fine views back of Pen-y-ghent and Ingleborough

Gate Cote Gill

Burned Hill

Gayle Beck

Low Gayle

Winshaw House

2. Path leaves track just beyond house to climb steeply over wet ground

Holme Hill

Roman Road

Gearstones outdoor centre

Far Gearstones

1. Right on track
FP Dent Head

To map 13B

From map 12B

alongside Great Knoutberry, heading towards Widdale and Hawes.

However, for a more adventurous walk above Dentdale, turn right for 400 metres when reaching the Dent road, until you reach the point where the Pennine Bridleway strikes due north across Newby Head.

This track is part of the ancient Galloway Gate drove road, used by Scottish drovers heading for Gearstones and Malham Moor. It is now a beautiful sunken track along the side of Wold Fell.

Follow the wall to the left until it descends to the track going through the moorland pass leading to Widdale and Hawes at Arten Gill.

Artengill Viaduct is actually built of local black marble. Near here there used to be a small quarry and stone-cutting machinery powered by a small waterwheel using water from the beck. In the 1830s a young man from Tyneside on his honeymoon on a walking and angling holiday became fascinated by the waterwheel. He decided it was a very inefficient way of converting water power to energy, and made detailed notes which he used to design the world's first turbine. The young man's name was William Armstrong (1810-1900), and he went on to become one of the greatest engineers of the 19th century, founder of the great Tyneside engineering dynasty, shipbuilders and armament manufacturers. His home at Cragside, Rothbury pioneered the use of domestic electricity.

Turn left through the gate on the Arten Gill track, then take the gate immediately on the right leading to the track which climbs steeply up the hillside towards Great Knoutberry, turning left with the track to head due westwards.

You now enjoy magnificent panoramic views from this track for the next mile and a half, following the contour above Dentdale as it curves below Great Knoutberry summit. You look directly across the narrow heads of the dale to Whernside, but on clear days down the whole of Dentdale towards Great Coum and the Howgill Fells, with even the first glimpse of Lakeland peaks beyond.

The track eventually joins the lane known (because of former coal pits on the high moorland) as the Coal Road. Turn left here, past Dodderham Moss plantation, down to Dent Station (an alternative point to end or start this part of the Dales Way).

If you are not catching a train, head down the winding road to the hamlet of Lea Yeat where you join the main Dales Way, along the footpath which leads from the far side of Lea Yeat Bridge.

Dent Station at 1,150 ft (460 metres) is the highest station on a main line railway in England and with its long views down the valley is a glorious place to start or end a walk. The stationmaster's house, on the station drive, built in 1876 in solid Midland Railway Derby Gothic style, was reputedly the first house in England to have double glazing, which anyone who has witnessed winter storms on the Settle-Carlisle line will understand. Over the severe winters of 1947 and 1963, trains were stranded here in snowdrifts for days (one old photograph shows only a locomotive chimney exposed). Even now the line struggles to remain open for freight and passenger trains in snowy weather. A line of almost ghostly, rotted sleepers still serves as a snow fence.

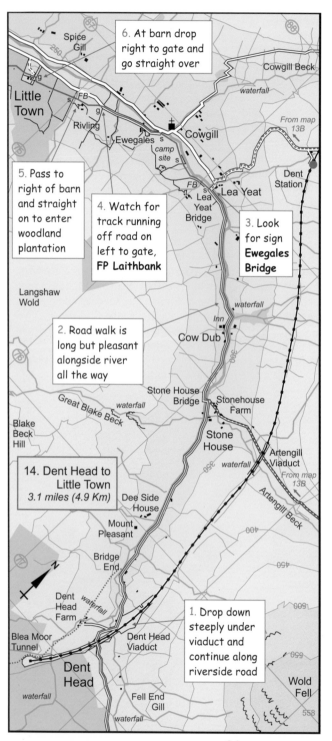

6. At barn drop right to gate and go straight over

5. Pass to right of barn and straight on to enter woodland plantation

4. Watch for track running off road on left to gate, FP Laithbank

3. Look for sign Ewegales Bridge

2. Road walk is long but pleasant alongside river all the way

14. Dent Head to Little Town
3.1 miles (4.9 Km)

1. Drop down steeply under viaduct and continue along riverside road

This part of the Dales Way follows the edge of the River Dee, which does not always run with visible water in many parts of Dentdale during drier times of the year. The limestone bed consists of a mass of underground fissures and cave systems into which the river retreats when water tables are low.

Dentdale's mild climate and its miles of hedgerows and dry stone walls make it an especially rewarding area for wildflowers early in the year. In spring, primroses, violets, pink campions and ragged robins are common in the verges, and the hedges are white with blackthorn, may blossom and dog rose, with the more vivid colours of scarlet hips, haws, rowans and blue-black sloes in autumn.

The path emerges at Ewegales Bridge below a camp site, and rejoins the back lane to Dent. A quarter of a mile along this lane, the Dales Way leaves the road on a path that may be a little difficult to find (follow waymarks and the map) heading below a small farmhouse at Rivling. The next stile takes you through a former coniferous plantation, now largely felled.

Keep ahead to Little Town, going below the
15 farm and back into the wood, and broadly contouring the hillside past Birchen Tree and below Hacker Gill. Pass Coat Faw, a fine railway age mansion, over stiles and then above walls across pastures to Clint, West Bank and Laithbank farms to rejoin the lane to Dent. About 200 metres along the lane, you turn right through the gate opposite Tub Hole, to a path across the field leading down into a little dip towards the river and a footbridge, Nelly Bridge.

The riverbed is often dry here in the summer months, the river flowing underground, leaving a few brown pools on the surface of the waterworn limestone.

Exactly who Nelly was is not known, but the Dales Way now follows the far side of the river alongside meadows, through gates or stiles, through four fields to the larger Tommy Bridge. Tommy and Nelly were surely related.

Cross Tommy Bridge, turning right to follow the Dales Way along

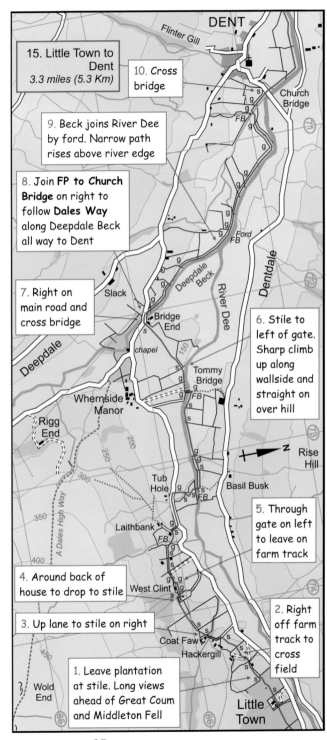

15. Little Town to Dent
3.3 miles (5.3 Km)

10. Cross bridge

9. Beck joins River Dee by ford. Narrow path rises above river edge

8. Join **FP to Church Bridge** on right to follow **Dales Way** along Deepdale Beck all way to Dent

7. Right on main road and cross bridge

6. Stile to left of gate. Sharp climb up along wallside and straight on over hill

5. Through gate on left to leave on farm track

4. Around back of house to drop to stile

3. Up lane to stile on right

2. Right off farm track to cross field

1. Leave plantation at stile. Long views ahead of Great Coum and Middleton Fell

DENT
Flinter Gill
Church Bridge
Deepdale Beck
River Dee
Dentdale
Ford
FB
Slack
Bridge End
chapel
Tommy Bridge
Whernside Manor
Rigg End
Deepdale
A Dales High Way
Tub Hole
Basil Busk
Rise Hill
Laithbank
West Clint
Coat Faw
Hackergill
Wold End
Little Town
150
200
250
300
350
400

the river to the next gate, but then bear left through a stile alongside a wall, keeping in the same direction to the summit of a small hillock.

There are splendid views down the dale from here. If you look at the landscape carefully you can see where it changes beyond the Dent Fault – a geological fault line roughly along Barbondale. To the north of the line, the landscape is dominated by the harder, darker exposed Silurian slates and shales more typical of the Lake District; to the south are the softer limestones and dark brown sandstones and gritstones of the southern and eastern Dales.

Cross the knoll down to the stile in the right hand wall corner. The cottage at Bridge End was once a knitting school. Turn right in the lane, but go first right again through a small gate to take the riverside path, marked by little pedestrian gates, which leads alongside Deepdale Beck, a tributary

of the Dee. The path eventually passes the confluence with the Dee. Keep straight ahead along the side of the Dee, usually flowing strongly here, to steps leading up to Church Bridge, the fine bridge below Dent Town.

Sedgwick memorial fountain (above) in Dent Main Street (below).

Dent and its Terrible Knitters

Dent, with its whitewashed cottages and narrow winding cobbled streets is one of the loveliest villages of the Dales, rich in character. The houses once had long balconies used by local people to chat to each other across Dent's narrow streets and courts as they knitted their socks and gloves. There is a handsome village church, rebuilt at the end of the 18th century, behind which, on the edge of the graveyard, is the 17th century grammar school, founded in 1607 and which served as the village school until 1897. The school's charitable foundation still supports local education-related good causes.

Dent remains the focal point in one of the most distinctive of the Yorkshire Dales. Facing westwards and sheltered by the hills, it enjoys a relatively mild climate, open to prevailing westerly winds and gentle rains, which to some degree explains its green and verdant nature.

Dentdale's small farms and narrow fields, some extending high up the fellside, reflect a pattern of settlement which is essentially Viking in origin and commentators have suggested that you would need to travel as far as Scandinavia or even Iceland to see a similar landscape. Dent is unlike typical Anglian valleys - for example Wharfedale with its clusters of villages – in that it has only has one township, Dent itself. When Dentdale was surveyed in 1793 as part of a report on the economic state of agriculture in England, in their account of this part of the old West Riding, the hard-headed surveyors described Dentdale as a dale "entirely surrounded by mountains" - and a "picture of terrestrial paradise".

Adam Sedgwick (1785-1874), the great field geologist and teacher, was born in Dent and went on to become Woodwardian professor of geology at Cambridge University for 55 years, mentor but later opponent of Charles Darwin, and a close friend of Prince Albert and Queen Victoria. Towards the end of his life, he wrote two pamphlets about his childhood in Dentdale in the late 18th century. The economy of the Dale at that time was sustained by hand knitting - stockings, gloves and hats - produced in vast quantities during almost every waking hour by men and women alike, whilst tending sheep, finishing household chores, or sitting round the fire singing traditional songs by candlelight. These were then sold on Kendal market.

But it was all about to change. The rapid mechanisation of the wool industry in the late 18th and early 19th century, especially the growth of the West Riding water and later steam powered wool mills with their techniques of mass manufacturing, totally destroyed the hand knitting industry. Within a few short years, the old self-sufficient community of owner–occupier farmers, the "statesmen" of Dent, was replaced by absentee landlords and tenant farmers. Poverty replaced prosperity, and the population of Dent Town declined over the next century by two-thirds as Dales people migrated to the growing manufacturing towns or even abroad.

Adam Sedgwick remained a great benefactor of the dale throughout his long life. After his death, a great boulder of polished Shap granite was carved, with his name, into a fountain in the village centre, a permanent tribute to Dent's greatest son.

A few hand knitting sheaths belonging to the terrible (i.e. frantic) knitters of Dent survive in local museums. The cottage near Mill Bridge, on the Dales Way east of the village, was a dame school where local children were taught the craft.

*The Sir Nigel Gresley crosses
Dent Head Viaduct (top).
Dropping into Dentdale (centre).
Sedbergh & the Howgills (bottom).*

16 The Dales Way actually crosses the road and continues along the river, but most Dales Way walkers will not wish to miss the cafes, pubs, village shop and creature comforts of Dent, a quarter of a mile up the hill.

To continue to Sedbergh, return to the riverside path either by walking back to Church Bridge or taking the path which leads past the car park and water treatment works to the riverside, turning left once again along the riverside path. This soon joins the road for a few yards, before leading through more small gates and fields on the right downstream to Barth Bridge. Cross the road and rejoin the riverside path on the far side at a stile. Then continue along the riverside through more small fields and gates, crossing a couple of small footbridges over streams before making your way up a short ascent. The path now goes through more gates and over a small footbridge before eventually joining the narrow back lane down the dale by Ellers Farm.

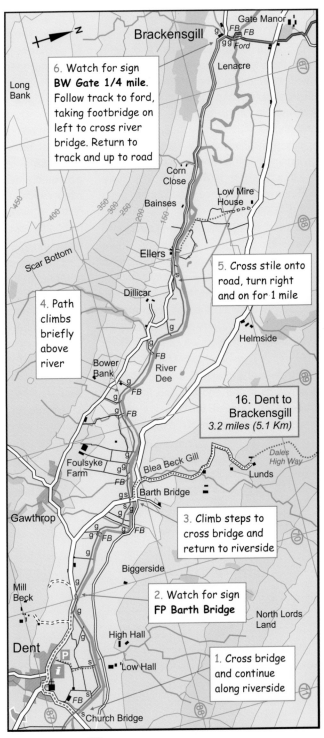

6. Watch for sign **BW Gate 1/4 mile.** Follow track to ford, taking footbridge on left to cross river bridge. Return to track and up to road

5. Cross stile onto road, turn right and on for 1 mile

16. Dent to Brackensgill
3.2 miles (5.1 Km)

4. Path climbs briefly above river

3. Climb steps to cross bridge and return to riverside

2. Watch for sign **FP Barth Bridge**

1. Cross bridge and continue along riverside

This is the point where the Dent Fault crosses Dentdale, on a line marked by Barbondale to the southwest and Helm Knot, the slightly craggy hillock across the river. Landscape and even vegetation changes subtly, and you will notice how the architecture of the buildings, both barns and houses – using hard local slate which is cut in a different way - also changes, giving the buildings and even walls more of a Lake District feel. There are more hedgerows in evidence than in other parts of the Dales.

Follow this quiet, traffic free lane for about a mile to the cottage at Brackensgill where the Dales Way turns sharp right along a track down to a footbridge, continuing up another enclosed track to the main road. 17 Cross and continue through the gateway slightly to the left, where a track climbs past Gate Cottage, turning left at a fork along another enclosed track past Gap Woods.

Climb over the crest of the hill, curving northwards to the end of Long Rigg; you then reach one of the most stunning viewpoints on the whole of the Dales Way.

A magnificent panorama across the whole of Sedbergh faces you; beyond is the huge backcloth of the Howgill Fells, the rounded summits of Winder, Crook and Knott dominating the view. These wonderful open hills offer some of the finest fell walking in the north of England with long open ridges to explore. Astonishingly, because of historic boundaries, most of the northern half of the Howgills is outside the national park boundary, but if current proposals by Natural England are accepted, this will soon be remedied in a major readjustment of the boundaries both of the Yorkshire Dales and Lake District National Parks.

Keep straight ahead on the track as it descends steeply to the hamlet of Millthrop, notable in the summer months for its cottage gardens brimming with flowers. Cross Millthrop Bridge, a fine 18th century stone arched bridge across the River Rawthey, where at the far side the Dales Way heads due westwards.

Most walkers, however, will head uphill to the attractive little town of Sedbergh, with its choice of shops, pubs, cafés and overnight accommodation. You can either follow the road, or part way up the hill, look for the fieldpath leading from a stile on the right. This takes you along an attractive path past the grounds of Sedbergh School directly to the town centre.

Middleton Fell

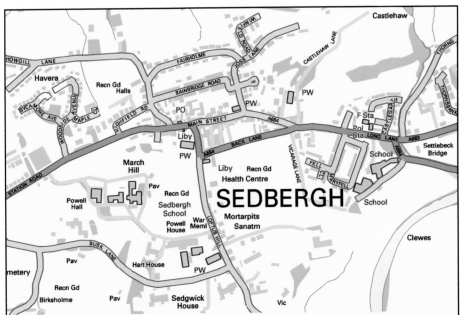

Sedbergh is a handsome town famed for its famous public school whose playing fields and buildings dominate the southern parts of the town. The town is very much, geographically and culturally, at a crossroads – looking south and east to the Yorkshire Dales of which it is very much a part. However, it is also a town whose architecture, including the use of local slates, has a strong Lake District feel, lying within Cumbria as well as the Yorkshire Dales National Park. It's the perfect place to explore the Howgills, and the town itself has friendly pubs, cafés, places to stay, and even a half-hidden Norman motte and bailey castle just above Joss Lane car park. There are also some intriguing 18th century courtyards, some with houses and workshops still retaining the typical Dentdale balconies.

The old grammar school

SEDBERGH TO BURNESIDE

This stage linking the north-west corner of the Dales and the edge of the Lake District is, at 16 miles, the longest on the Dales Way, but one of the most rewarding. It traverses a much quieter part of the Dales, Lunesdale, through undulating but attractive countryside between the two national parks, discovered by relatively few people except for Dales Way walkers. Much of the route is dominated by the massive and constant presence of the gloriously beautiful Howgill Fells, but as you climb out of the Lune Gorge, the spiky summits of the Lake District, with its contrasting geology and landscape, become increasingly apparent. The going is generally easy, and if staying at Sedbergh, a reasonably early start makes a teatime arrival at Burneside (with frequent transport links or a further 40 minutes' walk into Kendal).

The winding paths along riversides and through rolling pastureland can take time, but the views are magnificent throughout. If such a distance is a problem, you might divide your day neatly at Grayrigg which is served by a useful if irregular weekday bus between Tebay and Kendal, and there is also some accommodation in the Grayrigg/Patton area.

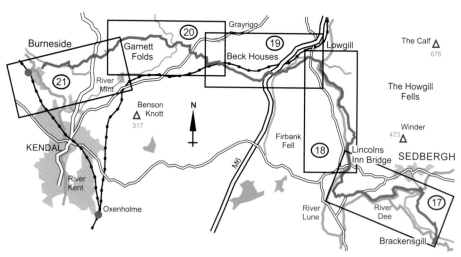

17 To get back onto the Dales Way, make your way back down to the river and to Millthrop Bridge, where the Dales Way continues through a small gate and grassy enclosure, climbing gently past trees and scattered woodland before returning to the riverside. You reach and follow a narrow lane past

Birks Mill, a former water-powered cotton mill.

Before reaching Birks, it is worth taking the detour using the well-signed footpath, through stiles and across the fields, crossing the line trackbed of the old Ingleton-Tebay railway line, to the little hamlet of Brigflatts, with its remarkable 17th century Quaker meeting house.

Sadly there is now no direct public path between Brigflatts and the Dales Way but you can walk up the access road from Brigflatts and turn left onto the A683 for a quarter of a mile to rejoin the Dales Way; alternatively, to avoid missing an attractive stretch of the route, return the way you came to the lane down to Birks Mill.

Ignore the footbridge at Birks Mill and continue on the Dales Way, soon reaching Waters' Meet, where the Rivers Dee and Rawthey merge, sparkling through the trees as the rushing waters blend.

The path emerges onto the busy A683. Now follows 500 metres of busy road walking (walk on the right to face oncoming traffic) until you reach the signed path on the right to High Oaks. The path descends to a little footbridge and crosses fields to the lovely early 18th century statesman's (yeoman's) house at High Oaks.

From here the Dales

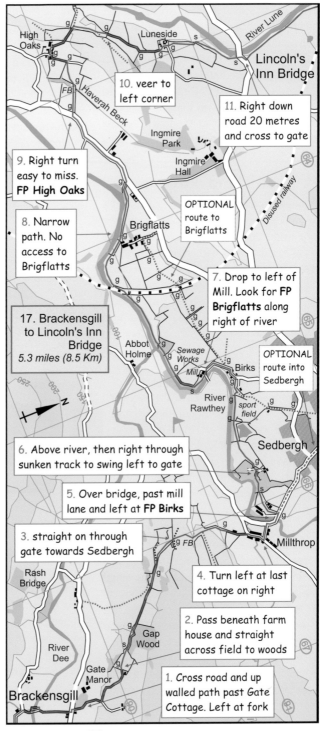

High Oaks

Luneside

River Lune

Lincoln's Inn Bridge

10. veer to left corner

FB

Haverah Beck

Ingmire Park

11. Right down road 20 metres and cross to gate

Disused railway

9. Right turn easy to miss. **FP High Oaks**

Ingmire Hall

OPTIONAL route to Brigflatts

8. Narrow path. No access to Brigflatts

Brigflatts

7. Drop to left of Mill. Look for **FP Brigflatts** along right of river

17. Brackensgill to Lincoln's Inn Bridge
5.3 miles (8.5 Km)

Abbot Holme

Sewage Works

Mill

Birks

OPTIONAL route into Sedbergh

River Rawthey

sport field

Sedbergh

6. Above river, then right through sunken track to swing left to gate

5. Over bridge, past mill lane and left at **FP Birks**

3. straight on through gate towards Sedbergh

FB

Millthrop

Rash Bridge

4. Turn left at last cottage on right

2. Pass beneath farm house and straight across field to woods

River Dee

Gap Wood

Gate Manor

Brackensgill

1. Cross road and up walled path past Gate Cottage. Left at fork

Way heads north and then north-eastwards, through a little spur of land between Lune and Rawthey. The path is well waymarked, marked by pedestrian gates as you turn into Lunesdale, passing Luneside Farm and through fields to Lincoln's Inn Bridge on the A684, though the inn that bequeathed its name to this old bridge has long since vanished. The Dales Way continues a short way to your right down this busy main road to a gate on the left.

Now follows a superb section of the Dales Way through the little known Lune Gorge – a delightful, seldom frequented valley which for centuries formed Yorkshire's far north-western boundary with the old county of Westmorland.

Brigflatts and Firbank Fell

Brigflatts and nearby Firbank Fell played a crucial role in the foundation of the worldwide Quaker movement. It was to the small flax weavers' settlement at Brigflatts that in the spring of 1652 George Fox made his way after his great vision on the summit of Pendle Hill, Lancashire. He travelled northwards through Wharfedale and Wensleydale before spending the night in Richard Robinson's house, the tall 17th century building at the entrance to the hamlet. Robinson was so suspicious of the stranger that he locked all the doors in case he was robbed during the night. It was on Firbank Fell, just three miles from the Dales Way, that Fox gave his famous open-air sermon to a thousand gathered Friends. This led to the founding of the Quaker movement.

Brigflatts Meeting House, a tiny and beautiful white cottage still in use after more than three centuries, was built as a labour of love and faith in 1675. The Friends, too poor to install a ceiling, lined the roof with moss, adding a gallery in 1711. A ceiling was finally constructed five years later. The cruel act of 1670 made nonconformist meetings illegal, and the Friends faced fear of imprisonment by the authorities. Believers came from a wide area around to remote Brigflatts, wearing nightcaps in case of arrest. Their fears were justified – in 1681 the Quakers of Dent were arrested and sent to Knaresborough, Wetherby and Pontefract gaols, and the practice continued throughout the 1680s. Sir John Otway, a Catholic local landowner and therefore familiar with the problems of a persecuted minority, frequently managed to get Friends out of gaol by requesting that they be released to help with the harvest. Perhaps they didn't return too quickly – or at all – Pontefract was a long way from Sedbergh. Sir John lived at Ingmire Hall, destroyed by fire in the 1820s.

It is hardly surprising that a faith like Quakerism flourished in the Sedbergh and Lunesdale area. As Wordsworth suggested, solitude, closeness of mountains and elemental forces of nature surely lend a seriousness and thoughtfulness to the most frivolous individual.

In later years Brigflatts acquired new fame, for the hamlet has given its name to the title of a fine autobiographical poem by Basil Bunting (1900-1985), the Northumbrian writer now regarded as one of the finest poets of his generation, who spent much of his teenage years in this area.

"Brag sweet tenor bull,
descant on Rawthey's madrigal"

Brigflatts (above).
Lune Viaduct (below).
View from Crook of Lune Bridge (right).

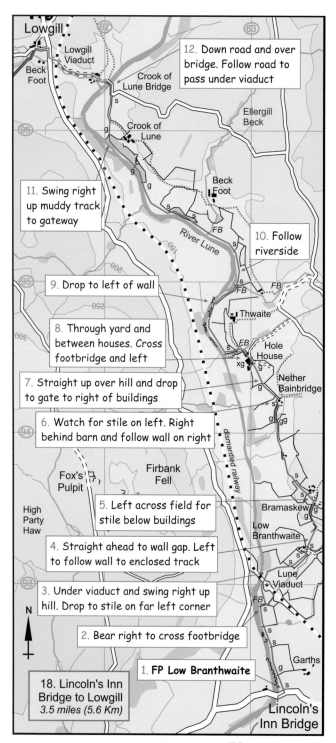

Lowgill

Lowgill
Viaduct

Beck
Foot

Crook of
Lune Bridge

Ellergill
Beck

Crook of
Lune

Beck
Foot

12. Down road and over bridge. Follow road to pass under viaduct

11. Swing right up muddy track to gateway

River Lune

FB

10. Follow riverside

9. Drop to left of wall

Thwaite

FB

8. Through yard and between houses. Cross footbridge and left

FB
Hole
House

xg

7. Straight up over hill and drop to gate to right of buildings

Nether
Bainbridge

6. Watch for stile on left. Right behind barn and follow wall on right

Fox's
Pulpit

Firbank
Fell

5. Left across field for stile below buildings

Bramaskew

Low
Branthwaite

High
Party
Haw

4. Straight ahead to wall gap. Left to follow wall to enclosed track

dismantled railway

3. Under viaduct and swing right up hill. Drop to stile on far left corner

N

Lune
Viaduct

FB

2. Bear right to cross footbridge

1. FP Low Branthwaite

Garths

18. Lincoln's Inn Bridge to Lowgill
3.5 miles (5.6 Km)

Lincoln's
Inn Bridge

The path passes though woods, past rapids and falls on the River Lune where the water is a deep whisky brown. Before reaching the railway viaduct turn right before a stream, Crosdale Beck, walking a hundred metres upstream to where a new footbridge has been constructed. Continue along the path and walk under the viaduct.

The Lune Viaduct, under which you pass, a magnificent structure of beautifully proportioned iron and brick that once carried the North Western railway across the Lune to Tebay, constitutes Victorian railway architecture at its best. It now broods over the valley like some extravagant folly, resembling a piece of the Crystal Palace erected in a place of solitude but richly deserving preservation.

The steep craggy hillside above the opposite side of the river is Firbank Fell. It was here, on an outcropping rock on the far side of this hill, (roughly in line with a tiny roadside chapel opposite) that George

Fox preached his great sermon to a thousand inspired followers in 1652. It is still known as Fox's Pulpit.

The Dales Way now heads to the right away from the river, through stiles to join tracks between and past Low Branthwaite and Bramaskew farms, through fields and gates (keep a look out for constant waymarks) to Nether Bainbridge and Hole House before turning back to the riverside. From here path finding is easier, though at times the path follows steep but pretty sections of hillside, wooded in places, but prone to landslip after heavy rain, the river rushing below you.

You eventually emerge in the lane just above Crook of Lune Bridge.

Crook of Lune Bridge, the most north-westerly tip of the old West Riding, is perhaps one of the most handsome of all the many narrow stone humpbacked 17th and 18th century bridges which so characterise the Dales Way. There are superb views northwards to the western slopes of the Howgills from here, reflected, when the river is calm, in the smooth waters of the River Lune.

Cross the bridge and go up the lane, under the huge Lowgill brick viaduct, turning right onto the road, then first left. But soon take a left turn (easy to miss) along a narrow track, over a stile and through a series of pastures above a shallow valley to Lakethwaite and beyond. As you ascend there are increasingly spectacular views back across the Howgill Fells and towards the foothills of the Lake District.

There are a couple more gates to negotiate below Lakethwaite before descending to a narrow lane, Old Scotch Road, the name suggesting a pre-turnpike packhorse way heading for the Borders through the Lune Gorge. Bear right off this lane along the path down to Lambrigg Head. The Dales

River Lune opposite Firbank Fell

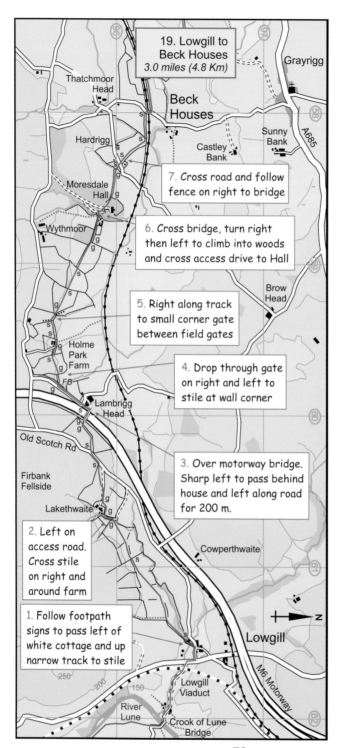

19. Lowgill to Beck Houses
3.0 miles (4.8 Km)

Thatchmoor Head

Beck Houses

Grayrigg

A685

Sunny Bank

Hardrigg

Castley Bank

7. Cross road and follow fence on right to bridge

Moresdale Hall

Wythmoor

6. Cross bridge, turn right then left to climb into woods and cross access drive to Hall

Brow Head

5. Right along track to small corner gate between field gates

Holme Park Farm

FB

4. Drop through gate on right and left to stile at wall corner

Lambrigg Head

Old Scotch Rd

Firbank Fellside

3. Over motorway bridge. Sharp left to pass behind house and left along road for 200 m.

Lakethwaite

Cowperthwaite

2. Left on access road. Cross stile on right and around farm

1. Follow footpath signs to pass left of white cottage and up narrow track to stile

250

290

150

Lowgill

Lowgill Viaduct

River Lune

Crook of Lune Bridge

M6 Motorway

N

Way leads to the bridge over the M6 at Lambrigg Head, before turning sharp left immediately after crossing the motorway towards Holme Park Farm.

Care with pathfinding is required here – landowners are not always as friendly to walkers as they are in other areas. Consult the map and check for waymarks as you go through stiles and gates, past Holme Park and over a series of stiles to pass in front of Moresdale Hall.

Cross the narrow lane near Hardrigg at a stile and follow the fence on your right, alongside the railway, turning right to cross the west coast main line with its high-speed tilting Pendolino trains heading to or from Scotland.

There are two options here: go along the lane past Beck Houses to the centre of Grayrigg village for return transport to Kendal or for accommodation. Otherwise turn sharp left and walk alongside the railway for 400 metres, before bearing right beside a small hillock and through a shallow valley. Then go

20

through gates past Green Head, turning right again along the access road from Grayrigg Foot to the main A685.

Cross here, the Dales Way taking the track towards Thursgill opposite before heading northwards through gates by Bracken Fold, descending the shallow valley of the River Mint to cross the stream at a footbridge and up to the gate into another farm access road. Turn right into the access road which goes below Shaw End, a fine early 19th century colonial style mansion, and continue to the lane.

Cross again, but here turn left in front of Biglands Farm to enter a long narrow field climbing gently up to Black Moss Tarn. More of a hill pond than a true mountain tarn, its waters, reflecting the sky, are usually filled with mallard and gulls.

Climb the hillock behind this little pool, passing under pylons to join the track past New House. Keep along this sunken track through gates heading towards Garnett Folds.

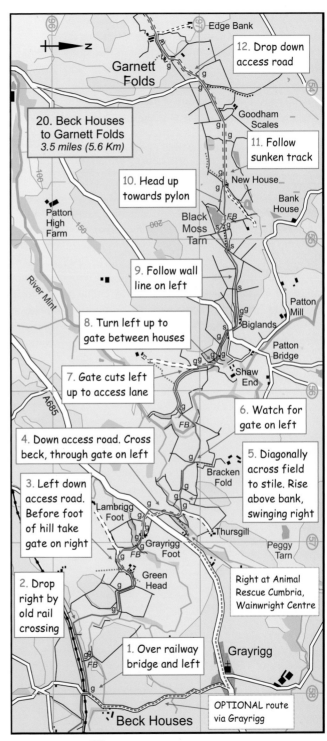

Garnett Folds

12. Drop down access road

20. Beck Houses to Garnett Folds
3.5 miles (5.6 Km)

11. Follow sunken track

10. Head up towards pylon

9. Follow wall line on left

8. Turn left up to gate between houses

7. Gate cuts left up to access lane

6. Watch for gate on left

4. Down access road. Cross beck, through gate on left

5. Diagonally across field to stile. Rise above bank, swinging right

3. Left down access road. Before foot of hill take gate on right

2. Drop right by old rail crossing

Right at Animal Rescue Cumbria, Wainwright Centre

1. Over railway bridge and left

Grayrigg

OPTIONAL route via Grayrigg

Beck Houses

Edge Bank
Goodham Scales
New House
Bank House
Patton High Farm
Black Moss Tarn
Patton Mill
Biglands
Patton Bridge
Shaw End
Bracken Fold
Lambrigg Foot
Thursgill
Peggy Tarn
Green Head
Grayrigg Foot
River Mint

79

When in 1845, James Cropper, the younger son of a prosperous local Quaker family, decided to set up in business as a paper manufacturer in two small Westmorland paper mills at Cowan Head and Burneside on the River Kent, he could have no idea that he was establishing one of the world's leading makers of specialist paper and high-performance nonwoven materials. The story of what is now **James Cropper plc** is a truly remarkable one –

survival in an increasingly competitive world by constantly adapting to keep ahead of that competition. This has included the development of a huge range of specialist papers, including brilliantly coloured and textured papers and card used globally for high quality artwork, book production, design and retail packaging. But in the 21st century, Croppers have adapted their paper-making technology to produce Technical Fibres, from glass, carbon, aramid, polyester and thermoplastics, used throughout the world in the aeronautical and aerospace industries, as well as in many hundreds of practical applications and cutting edge technology. Though now a multi-million pound business, much of it devoted to exports, with a highly skilled local workforce, the expanded Burneside Mills, still stewarded by the Cropper family, are operated to the highest environmental standards. This proves that conservation of the countryside such as that along the Dales Way and supporting a vibrant local community can go hand-in-hand with world beating industrial manufacturing technology.

Aerial photo of Burneside and the Paper Mill, looking NE. Tenement Farm is at the top of the picture.

21 Easy walking now, following the access road past Skelsmergh Tarn and Tarn Bank to eventually reach the A6.

Still designated the A6, this now relatively quiet road was once the main arterial road between England and Scotland. It is a road with a rich and at times stormy history, as long and as complicated as the relationship between the two countries it still serves. It has been used by countless travellers on foot, on horseback and by stage coach between England and the Scottish Borders throughout the centuries, as well as by endless lines of trundling carriers' carts carrying goods, chattels and less affluent passengers. Towns along the route, such as Kendal, Shap and Penrith flourished as key staging posts, with busy inns where horses could be changed and travellers could eat or spend a night.

The road was at various times the military route used by both Scottish invaders and English armies. It was used by the Jacobites under the leadership of Charles Stewart, the Young Pretender, in their ill-fated rebellion of 1745

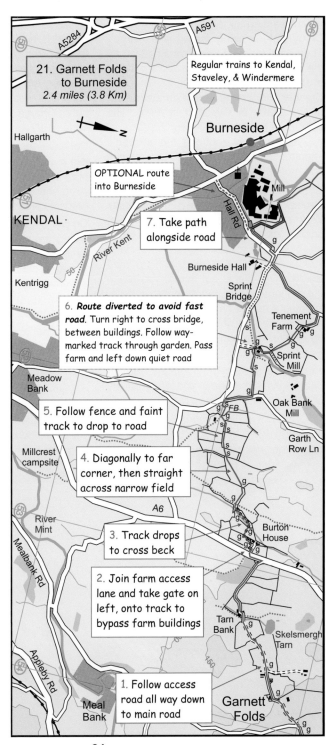

21. Garnett Folds to Burneside
2.4 miles (3.8 Km)

Regular trains to Kendal, Staveley, & Windermere

Burneside

Hallgarth

OPTIONAL route into Burneside

Mill

KENDAL

7. Take path alongside road

River Kent

Burneside Hall

Kentrigg

Sprint Bridge

6. *Route diverted to avoid fast road.* Turn right to cross bridge, between buildings. Follow way-marked track through garden. Pass farm and left down quiet road

Tenement Farm

Sprint Mill

Meadow Bank

Oak Bank Mill

5. Follow fence and faint track to drop to road

FB

Garth Row Ln

Millcrest campsite

4. Diagonally to far corner, then straight across narrow field

A6

River Mint

3. Track drops to cross beck

Burton House

Mealbank Rd

2. Join farm access lane and take gate on left, onto track to bypass farm buildings

Tarn Bank

Skelsmergh Tarn

Appleby Rd

1. Follow access road all way down to main road

Meal Bank

Garnett Folds

which reached as far as Manchester and Derby before being forced into retreat. They were pursued back into Scotland by the English general, Prince William, Duke of Cumberland, later known as "Butcher" Cumberland, before their eventual defeat at the Battle of Culloden in 1746. The opening of the Lancaster-Penrith section of the M6 in 1970 reduced the strategic importance of the road which now carries little more than relatively local traffic.

Cross the A6, turning left, then first right through Burton House farmyard. The Dales Way now meanders through a series of small fields, through a combination of gates and stiles, before reaching the narrow lane that leads to Oak Bank Mill. Turn right towards Oak Bank, but before you reach the cottages, turn left through a gate, keeping a hedge on your left as you walk down to the side of the little River Sprint - really little more than a stream.

The Dales Way originally followed this streamside path to Sprint Bridge, turning right along the narrow and dangerously busy lane which carries far more traffic than it should as it is a popular rat-run for speeding local drivers. The new route crosses the bridge at Sprint Mill, between buildings, bearing right along a waymarked footpath through a pretty garden area. A stile leads into a field with a wall on the left, following this to a large metal gate. The way continues west, with the wall now on the right, through a couple of gates to pass Tenement Farm.

Continue out along the farm access road to join a quiet country lane, left, down to the busy road near a junction. A right and left bring you quickly onto Hall Road and the roadside path down towards Burneside.

On your left is Burneside Hall, a pele tower dating back to the 14th century, built to keep marauding Scots at bay. It forms a fine example of a semi-fortified house with a crenellated tower and the remains of an impressive gateway. Keep ahead into Burneside village centre.

Burneside is an industrial village on the River Kent with an inn, a shop and otherwise few visitor facilities, though there is some accommodation in the village. The railway station at the far side of the village has hourly trains into Kendal and there is also a frequent bus service – or if you are not too footsore it's a two-mile road walk.

Sprint Mill

BURNESIDE TO BOWNESS

The final stage of the Dales Way is no anticlimax. It starts gently enough along the meandering River Kent, and soon moves through the foothills of the Lake District as it enters the national park, building up, with a growing sense of anticipation, to a dramatic viewpoint where the Lakeland peaks stretch out around you in a magnificent panorama. The route then winds its way through attractive parkland and scattered woods to finish at the Dales Way seat above the village of Bowness or, if you choose, the pebbled shore of Windermere itself.

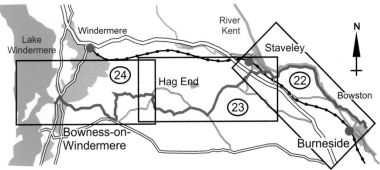

22 To continue along the Dales Way from Burneside, return along Hall Lane to where the Dales Way goes through a pedestrian gate to follow an enclosed path behind Cropper's Mill.

James Cropper (1823-1900) established his paper mill at Burneside in 1845 to take advantage of the copious water supplies along the fast flowing River Kent fed by the high rainfall on nearby mountain slopes. In spite of his industrial background, Cropper was an early campaigner for the preservation of the Lakeland landscape, who eventually became Liberal MP for Kendal.

The Dales Way continues upstream alongside the Kent, through fields and across stiles to join the lane from Laithwaite Farm and the bridge across the river. Cross here, turning right along the lane to Bowston, but taking the enclosed path on the right, signed Dales Way to Staveley, which goes upstream past Bowston Weir, then along the access road to Cowan Head, another former mill complex consisting of an 18th century mill building and attendant mill workers' cottages now converted to residential cottages and apartments.

Beyond Cowan Head the Dales Way follows another very attractive stretch of open riverside above the mill weir, through gates and over stiles, rising slightly before following the river upstream as it twists round a small headland. It then passes the delightfully named Beckmickle Ing, with Spring Hag Wood across the other side of the river.

Although there are no formal signs, you are now entering the Lake District National Park.

Follow the riverside path through stiles and pedestrian gates as the Kent curves westwards, eventually emerging on the main road just above Staveley. Turn right along the pavement towards Staveley village.

Staveley is a compact residential village where the little River Gowan meets the

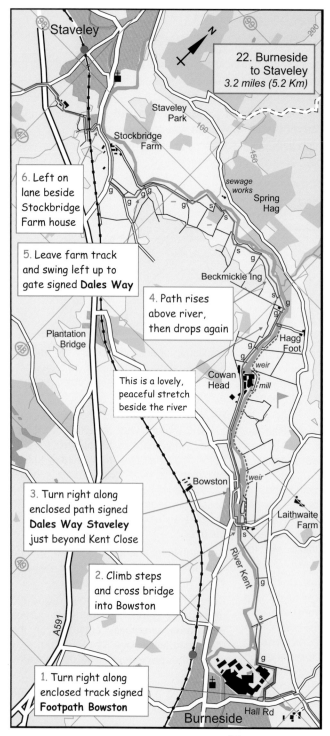

Staveley

22. Burneside to Staveley
3.2 miles (5.2 Km)

Staveley Park

Stockbridge Farm

sewage works

Spring Hag

6. Left on lane beside Stockbridge Farm house

5. Leave farm track and swing left up to gate signed **Dales Way**

Beckmickle Ing

4. Path rises above river, then drops again

Plantation Bridge

Hagg Foot

This is a lovely, peaceful stretch beside the river

weir

Cowan Head

mill

3. Turn right along enclosed path signed **Dales Way Staveley** just beyond Kent Close

Bowston

weir

Laithwaite Farm

2. Climb steps and cross bridge into Bowston

River Kent

A591

1. Turn right along enclosed track signed **Footpath Bowston**

Hall Rd

Burneside

Kent. The conservation area at the heart of the village is dominated by the fine 14th century St Margaret's Tower in the main street - the surviving fragment of the medieval church which was replaced by the modern church of St James in 1865. While St James's may not have the antiquity of its predecessor, it boasts a fine east window designed by the celebrated Pre-Raphaelite artist Edward Burne-Jones and executed by the poet-craftsman William Morris.

The village caters for Dales Way walkers with a shop, toilets, buses, a railway station with trains to Kendal, Oxenholme and Windermere and a couple of inns, one of which, slightly incongruously, is situated in the village's industrial estate at the northern end of the village. Here you'll find the award-winning Hawkshead Brewery's beer hall - the brewery tap – linked to a cafe next door where you can enjoy a full range of their Cumbrian craft ales and food.

If you are not walking into Staveley, the Dales Way continues on the track on the left some

23

100 metres beyond Stockbridge Farm, leading underneath the single-track Windermere branch railway. Turn right beyond the tunnel, following the path past Moss Side Farm and out along the farm drive to the road from Staveley, just before the bridge over the busy A591 Staveley by-pass.

About 180 metres past the bridge, what looks like a house entrance by the hedge on the right takes the Dales Way past Field Close and left through a gate to join a field path which bears right across a field and up a long sloping path through more fields. Behind you as you climb are increasingly fine views back towards the hills. Go through several gates to finally emerge on a narrow lane or access road opposite New Hall Farm.

Turn right to follow this very quiet lane as it curves up the hillside. Again there are splendid views back towards the Howgills sweeping around in a huge panorama to the craggier Lakeland peaks ahead.

The lane descends into a hollow where, near the evocatively named

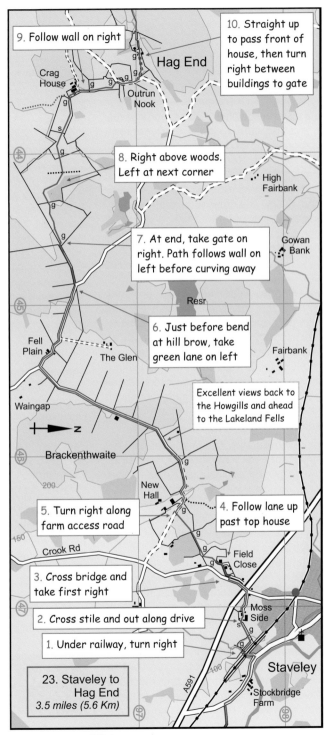

9. Follow wall on right

10. Straight up to pass front of house, then turn right between buildings to gate

Hag End

Crag House

Outrun Nook

8. Right above woods. Left at next corner

High Fairbank

7. At end, take gate on right. Path follows wall on left before curving away

Gowan Bank

Resr

6. Just before bend at hill brow, take green lane on left

Fairbank

Fell Plain

The Glen

Excellent views back to the Howgills and ahead to the Lakeland Fells

Waingap

Brackenthwaite

New Hall

5. Turn right along farm access road

4. Follow lane up past top house

Crook Rd

Field Close

3. Cross bridge and take first right

Moss Side

2. Cross stile and out along drive

1. Under railway, turn right

Staveley

23. Staveley to Hag End
3.5 miles (5.6 Km)

Stockbridge Farm

A591

The Lake District National Park

The Lake District is England's largest national park, covering just over 910 square miles of spectacular mountain and lake scenery. This remarkable landscape is the result of complex geological processes. Elevation and exposure of ancient, contorted and eroded slates and granites in this part of Cumbria have produced England's highest mountains and longest and deepest lakes. Fast flowing streams and rivers, fed from mountain tarns by heavy rainfall, cascade through valleys or dales already deeply carved by glaciation. Assisted by high rainfall, the dales support a rich natural eco-system, the steep valley sides dominated by semi-natural woodlands, especially birch and oak woods, the many crags covered with different varieties of mosses and lichens. The high mountain pastures and crags also provide good habitat for birds of prey. This is one of the few places in England where the golden eagle is still to be seen, as well as ospreys and hen harriers, and even along this part of the Dales Way buzzards and kestrels are common.

Human influence has also shaped this landscape, as evidenced by prehistoric dwellings and enclosures, Roman roads and encampments, and countless medieval farmsteads and settlements, many still occupied. Centuries of farming along the narrow valleys has resulted in the tough breed of sheep known as Herdwicks, which still dominate the higher hill pastures. In times past, local people used red lead to weatherproof the outside of their houses which was then covered with limewash to create the characteristic white farmhouses and cottages which are such a traditional feature of the Lake District. The great open common lands which cover so much of the mountainside and moorland have long enjoyed full access rights for walkers. Many of these commons are owned and managed by the National Trust, now a principal landowner in the Lake District.

But the Lake District's claim to international fame is as the birthplace of the English Romantic Movement, and of the great walker-poet William Wordsworth (1770-1850), whose poems first captured the essence of this spectacular landscape. Wordsworth was a great champion of footpaths and rights of way, and even wrote one of the first - and best - guide books to the Lake District in 1810. With his many followers, he helped to create the taste for wild, mountain landscapes and a passion for walking in them - a worldwide phenomenon that persists to this day. In a later edition of his guide, Wordsworth suggested that the Lake District should be regarded as "a sort of national property, in which every man has a right and interest who has an eye to perceive and a heart to enjoy" - the first time that the concept of a national park had ever been suggested. However, it was not until over 100 years later, in 1951, that the Lake District National Park was finally formally designated, well after the world's first national park in Yellowstone, USA, in 1872. Every walker of the Dales Way owes William Wordsworth a great debt of gratitude.

With something like eight million visitors a year, careful management is needed to safeguard many of the popular walks and climbs in the national park. Thankfully the Dales Way runs through one of the quietest corners of the national park, where walkers are unlikely to have to queue at stiles or to find footpaths severely eroded.

Waingap, you join another lane from Crook. Turn right here, again climbing uphill for about a quarter of a mile till you reach a fork, where you turn left along an unsurfaced track. Where the track ends, take care to take the gate on the right (signed) which leads into open pasture with several exposed crags forming a little hillock – a good picnic place. The Dales Way follows the faint track below these crags, bearing right to descend through a gate by a wood. Keep right to go alongside the wood past gorse bushes, before going left at the next corner, through gates and stiles, across a little hollow with its mysterious spring before climbing up to Crag House Farm. Keep right, following waymarks through the gates below the farm, then through more gates up to the lane opposite the pretty farmhouse at Outrun Nook.

Turn right in this lane and follow it uphill to the lane corner, where you go left along the track to Hag End Farm.

24 The Dales Way winds between the buildings and climbs through a little gate to follow a path that leads through a pass or saddle between the low, craggy hills, with the minor peak of Grandsire (251 metres) just to your immediate right.

Pause as you reach this spectacular viewpoint to admire the great panorama of hills – you feel you have truly arrived in the Lake District. If the weather is clear, you can see Black Combe away to the left, the Coniston Fells, Crinkle Crags, Bowfell, with Scafell and Scafell Pike (England's highest peaks) just visible beyond. Moving your gaze around you see the Langdale Pikes, Fairfield, Stony Cove Pike and the Kentmere Fells, with

School Knott, another fine viewpoint accessible by footpath, close ahead.

Easy walking down from here to Windermere, though a little care is needed. Follow the path down and to the right, to the natural gap between Grandsire and School Knott, heading left to cross through fields and alongside a wall to reach a stony track. Take care not to go straight ahead here through Pinethwaite, but turn sharp left (look for signs), heading due south along this track, through field gates. This eventually passes the group of farm buildings and houses at Cleabarrow, keeping ahead above a small pond to the main B5284 Windermere-Crook road opposite Windermere Golf Course.

Do not go onto this busy road, but cross the wallgap on the right, which takes you onto a short enclosed path along the side of the wall for about 150 metres before you turn right along another lane. Pass to the left of the house, through gates to climb uphill through trees. Then drop to cross a road, and keep ahead to where the path drops to meet the lane by Matson Ground.

The Dales Way goes straight across this lane and continues along a track through gates and above a large pond by Home Farm, usually full of fascinating local and more exotic wildfowl. Bear slightly left at the end of the pond. Look out for the gate which takes you behind the hedge to a track, then a second gate on the left (all well waymarked) leading across a field and along another enclosed way past Brantfell Farm, where a lovely sloping path by trees descends to the final moment of glory – the stone Dales Way seat, the twin of the one you started from in Ilkley.

This seat at the end of the Dales Way is a

For those who walk the DALESWAY

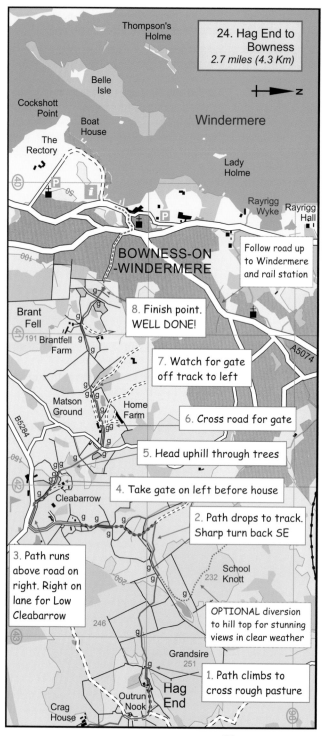

24. Hag End to Bowness
2.7 miles (4.3 Km)

N

Thompson's Holme

Belle Isle

Cockshott Point

Boat House

The Rectory

Windermere

Lady Holme

Rayrigg Wyke

Rayrigg Hall

BOWNESS-ON -WINDERMERE

Follow road up to Windermere and rail station

Brant Fell

191 Brantfell Farm

8. Finish point. WELL DONE!

A5074

7. Watch for gate off track to left

Matson Ground

Home Farm

6. Cross road for gate

5. Head uphill through trees

4. Take gate on left before house

Cleabarrow

2. Path drops to track. Sharp turn back SE

3. Path runs above road on right. Right on lane for Low Cleabarrow

School Knott

232

OPTIONAL diversion to hill top for stunning views in clear weather

246

Grandsire

251

1. Path climbs to cross rough pasture

Hag End

Outrun Nook

Crag House

magnificent viewpoint; as you gaze over the rooftops and trees of Bowness and across the great dark glacial valley, there is a glimpse of Windermere itself, glistening against its background of densely wooded hills and dotted with the white sails of yachts.

But for many Dales Way walkers this isn't quite the end. Stroll through the metal gate below the Dales Way seat and walk down Brantfell Road, past the Royal Oak, which claims to be the last - or first - inn on the Dales Way, and into the town of Bowness-on-Windermere. Head right, then first left past St Martin's Church to the lakeside promenade. Then, ignoring the crowds, make for the side of the little wooden boathouse, where you can walk on the shingle and ceremoniously dip your boots into the waters of the lake.

For most Dales Way walkers, to reach the edge of this huge, shimmering lake is a very special moment, a sense of achievement that, mingled with memories of the many wonderful, varied landscapes you have walked through, will never leave you.

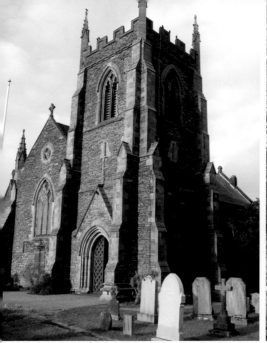

St. Oswald's Church, Burneside (top left). Dales Way near Brackenthwaite, Staveley (top right). Windermere from School Knott (bottom).

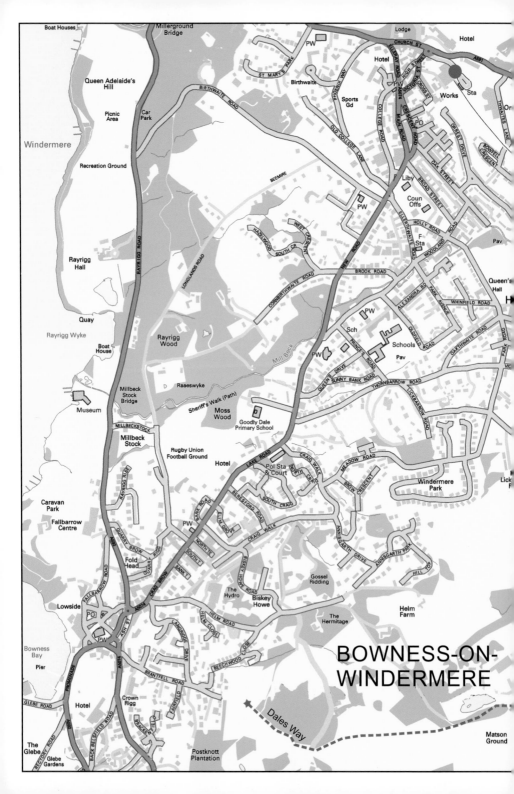

BOWNESS-ON-WINDERMERE

Windermere, England's greatest lake, is 17 kilometres (10½ miles) long, and in its deepest places some 67 metres deep. It is set against an impressive background of thickly wooded hills, with the higher peaks stretching into the background. The lake has no fewer than 18 islands, the largest being the privately owned Belle Isle reached by boat trips in the summer.

Despite problems of pollution caused by users of the lake and run-off from lakeside settlements, Windermere is a rich natural environment, home not only to the more familiar pike, perch and trout, but also the char, once a local delicacy, but now quite rare. Recent attempts to improve water quality and marine habitat have resulted in a major research centre being established at Lakeside, on the southern tip of the lake, which also has a magnificent aquarium where local and more exotic species are on display. A recent controversial but for most very welcome 10mph speed limit, imposed by the National Park Authority, has reduced intrusive noise from powerboats and made life easier for sailing boats on this most important of English lakes.

There has long been confusion about the name of Windermere, which historically belongs to the lake and not the town. The town was a creation of the railway age when, in 1847, the Kendal-Windermere railway branch line was opened from the Lancaster-Carlisle railway and terminated at two tiny hamlets, Applethwaite and Birthwaite. These were hardly names to attract potential tourists to the glories of the lake, so the town with its many hotels and guesthouses which rapidly grew around the station took the more marketable name of its nearby lake, even though steep gradients prevented the railway from actually reaching the waterside. Horse-drawn waggonettes and later motor buses were required for visitors to reach the lake. In 1869, however, the rival Furness Railway built a separate branch line from Ulverston to jetties on the shore. This branch, now an isolated 3½ miles of track, still carries the Haverthwaite-Lakeside steam railway whose vintage trains meet the Windermere boats.

Windermere has long been a major transport route as many archaeological remains testify, but since the coming of the railway, the lake has been criss-crossed by leisure boat services, most notably those of the Windermere Iron Steamboat Company, which since 1848 have cruised majestically along the entire length of the lake between Lakeside, Bowness and Ambleside.

Bowness-on-Windermere is a far older settlement than Windermere itself, though the two have long since merged in almost continuous ribbon development. Old houses and inns, winding streets and a handsome 15th century church still survive at the heart of this inland tourist resort - one of the busiest and more popular in the British Isles, enjoying well over a million visitors a year.

There's certainly everything in Bowness the weary Dales Way wanderer needs – food, accommodation, refreshment, tourist information, excellent return transport services – a frequent local bus will take you the mile and a half up the hill to Windermere Station for regular buses to Kendal and Lancaster, or trains to Oxenholme, Lancaster (connections to Leeds for Ilkley), and almost anywhere else in England.

Or you may wish to spend a few more days exploring the glories of the Lake District: maybe heading off on the Windermere-Hawkshead Ferry towards Coniston to pick up the Cumbria Way to Keswick or Carlisle; maybe walking the 45-mile Windermere Way around the Lake; or maybe just enjoying a little relaxation and gentle pottering among the crags and lakes that were the birthplace of English Romanticism.

Wharfe valley from Bank Top, Arthington (above).
Looking back to the Chevin from Burley Moor
(below). The Bradford Link starts at the cathedral
gates in the city centre (right).

Link route maps shown at a scale of 1:50,000

The Leeds Link

21 miles (34 km)

The concept of extending the Dales Way from the centre of Leeds lay at the heart of what the Dales Way has always been about. Whilst it was recognised that most Dales Way walkers would want to start in Ilkley at the very edge of the Yorkshire Dales, the idea of a walk "from Woodhouse Moor to Windermere" was always an inspiring thought, linking on foot the great city of Leeds with England's foremost national park, and enjoying a long walk through the heart of the magnificent Yorkshire Dales in the process.

The full route is 21 miles but for most walkers, the parallel bus between Ilkley, Otley, Bramhope and Leeds, or train service from Menston and Ilkley, makes dividing the route into two more comfortable day stages of about 10 miles an easy task.

Leeds, in Lower Airedale, lies on the foothills of the Pennines. The growth of the essentially Victorian industrial city has almost, but not quite, eradicated traces of the former Tudor trading town situated at

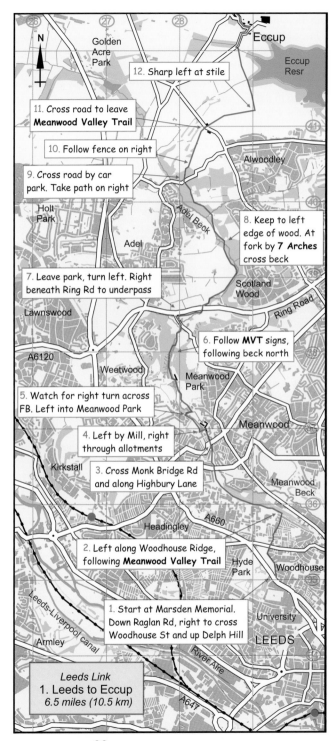

Eccup

12. Sharp left at stile

11. Cross road to leave **Meanwood Valley Trail**

10. Follow fence on right

9. Cross road by car park. Take path on right

8. Keep to left edge of wood. At fork by **7 Arches** cross beck

7. Leave park, turn left. Right beneath Ring Rd to underpass

6. Follow **MVT** signs, following beck north

5. Watch for right turn across FB. Left into Meanwood Park

4. Left by Mill, right through allotments

3. Cross Monk Bridge Rd and along Highbury Lane

2. Left along Woodhouse Ridge, following **Meanwood Valley Trail**

1. Start at Marsden Memorial. Down Raglan Rd, right to cross Woodhouse St and up Delph Hill

Leeds Link
1. Leeds to Eccup
6.5 miles (10.5 km)

the highest navigable point of the River Aire, at Leeds Bridge, where hand-woven *pieces* of cloth could be traded with merchants who came along the Humber and Aire rivers from the east coast ports.

Even to this day, a short stretch of cobbled Kendal Lane behind Clarendon Road indicates where the old highway to Kendal, a textile and market town once more important than Leeds, came into the city, a route several centuries older than the Dales Way.

You can of course start the walk in the centre of Leeds, in City Square or at the Town Hall, but Woodhouse Moor, an ancient piece of common land, now a popular town park close to cafes, pubs and bedsit terraced houses beloved by generations of university students, makes a good point to start a country walk. The official starting point is

The Marsden statue

the stone statue of Henry Marsden (1823-1876) at the city centre end of Woodhouse Moor. A local philanthropist and popular mayor of Leeds (1872-1875), he would surely have approved of the Leeds Dales Way Link.

The official Dales Way route follows the Meanwood Valley Trail (a later creation) which goes onto Woodhouse Ridge via Rampart Road and Delph Lane, but a more interesting route is to follow the edge of Woodhouse Moor to Hyde Park Corner, but turn right before the traffic lights into Cliff Road, then left into Cliff Lane, looking for a narrow enclosed alleyway or ginnel between high stone walls, behind gardens. This crosses Grosvenor Mount and Grosvenor Road into Devonshire Road, at the end of which it continues into Woodhouse Ridge, another stretch of woodland in a small, narrow park above the Meanwood Valley.

Meanwood Valley is an astonishing survival from pre-industrial and early industrial Leeds, a steeply sided tributary valley of the River Aire, with much surviving ancient Pennine woodland, remains of old water-powered and later steam-powered mills, even an urban farm, and two popular parks.

Head downhill in the same direction, past a couple of iron posts and over a bridge to cross Grove Lane, bearing slightly left keeping Meanwood Beck on your right, into Brookfield Road, over Monk Bridge Road, along Highbury Lane. Turn left by the old mill with its fine chimney, then right by the allotments, looking for the right turn over a footbridge into Meanwood Park.

Follow the Meanwood Valley Trail along Meanwood Beck through Meanwood Park, turning right then left past former mill cottages known as Hustlers Row, closely following the side of the beck and its attendant mill race, through woods. At the far end of the park the path joins Parkside Road and heads for the alarmingly busy A6120 Leeds Ring Road. Look for the track to the right which parallels the main road and leads to an underpass to emerge in Adel Woods.

Follow the well-used path through lovely oak, hawthorn and bluebell woods, a popular Leeds beauty spot. The stream below you is now known as Adel Beck. Keep to the left-hand side of the wood, above the stream. Where you reach a fine stone aqueduct supported by seven round arches, cross the beck and continue on a high path above the steep valley, heading due north. Look out for a tiny stone carved fountain or spring alongside the path, possibly medieval in origin, and known locally as the Slobbering Baby.

The path finally emerges on Stairfoot Lane near the car park. Cross, turn right to join the continuation of the path on the left which follows a fence by woodland, then alongside the golf course, finally reaching busy King Lane. Take care to avoid often dangerously fast traffic here.

Cross and continue along the path to the right of Golf Farm, then descend gently across a couple of fields before turning left to cross a shallow gully at the head of Eccup Reservoir heading back up the hillside to a shallow valley where you join Eccup Moor Road. Turn right towards Eccup village.

It is amazing to think that this unspoiled, still very rural village is within the boundary of the city of Leeds. The reservoir at Eccup supplying Leeds dates from 1843, a time when fresh water was beginning to be seen as vital for public health. Red kites are often seen in the vicinity.

Follow the lane which runs left from the village past Thorn Bush Farm up to Brooklands Farm. Unless you are visiting the popular New Inn, some 400 metres along Eccup Lane, take the path through the farmyard past Brooklands. Keep directly ahead over a stile before bearing left to the low summit of Bowshaws Ash, beyond which you soon turn sharp right to descend towards Bank Side Farm.

This is the first magnificent viewpoint along the Dales Way, with panoramic views across Lower Wharfedale spread out below you: the town of Otley to the left, Arthington Viaduct carrying the Leeds-Harrogate railway sweeping away into the distance and Almscliff Crag beyond.

At Bank Side turn left along the track, Bank Top Lane, to Bank Top Farm. From here cross Arthington Lane, and follow the path alongside the fence, bearing slightly left to join the tarmac lane, Breary Lane East, to West Breary. Keep ahead to the cross roads and the centre of Bramhope. The bus stop back to Leeds lies to your right.

Bramhope is a large pleasant dormitory village for Leeds commuters, with some fine suburban houses. Its greatest claim to fame, perhaps, is the simple Puritan chapel at the top of the village, built in 1649 by local landowners, the Dynley family. It is a rare example of a chapel built in the Commonwealth period and contains its original furnishings, including a fine three-decker pulpit.

Cross to continue along Breary Lane and Eastgate round the back of the village, past the crossroads (Fox & Hounds pub and toilets on the right) to the edge of the village where a stile on the right leads to a field path, marked by stiles, which soon bears left to houses at Hilton Edge on the main A658 Harrogate Road above Pool Bank.

Cross the road with extreme care. The Dales Way now heads into Caley Deer Park, which forms part of the magnificent Chevin Forest Park.

The Chevin, a wooded ridge which dominates the skyline to the south of Otley, is a major Lower Wharfedale landmark, its woodland now owned and managed by Leeds City Council as one of the city's finest open spaces. The Danefield Estate, which covers most of the Chevin, was given to the people of Otley in 1952 by Major Horton-Fawkes, a local landowner of nearby Farnley Hall, as a memorial to the many local people who had died in the second world war. With its spectacular sandstone crags, its oak, beech and sycamore woods and coniferous plantations, the area is noted for its birdlife, both resident and migratory, including woodcock, goldcrest and redstart. There is also a small population of roe deer.

Once in the main woodland, follow the Dales Way waymarks right, descending to another crossing of paths, where the Dales Way heads left along the ridge through

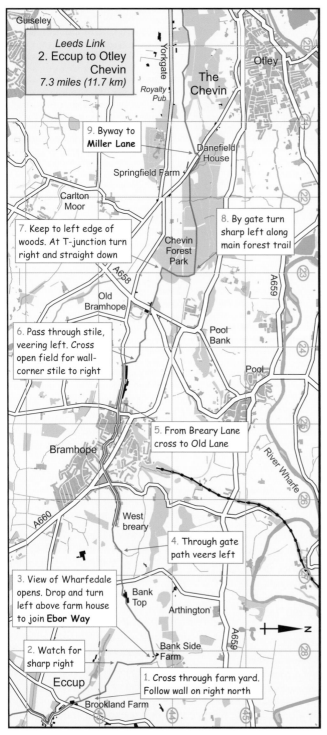

Leeds Link
2. Eccup to Otley Chevin
7.3 miles (11.7 km)

Guiseley

Otley

Yorkgate

Royalty Pub

The Chevin

9. Byway to **Miller Lane**

Danefield House

Springfield Farm

Carlton Moor

7. Keep to left edge of woods. At T-junction turn right and straight down

8. By gate turn sharp left along main forest trail

Chevin Forest Park

A658

Old Bramhope

6. Pass through stile, veering left. Cross open field for wall-corner stile to right

Pool Bank

Pool

A659

5. From Breary Lane cross to Old Lane

Bramhope

River Wharfe

West breary

4. Through gate path veers left

A660

3. View of Wharfedale opens. Drop and turn left above farm house to join **Ebor Way**

Bank Top

Arthington

2. Watch for sharp right

Bank Side Farm

A659

Eccup

1. Cross through farm yard. Follow wall on right north

N

Brookland Farm

Caley Deer Park to reach East Chevin Road at Lower Shawfield car park. Turn right here (a narrow path parallels the road) for 200 metres before crossing the road and taking an enclosed track which leads up to the well named Surprise View on the summit of the Chevin – another splendid viewpoint looking across the whole of Lower Wharfedale, with Otley below. The Royalty Inn lies on York Gate, just beyond the car park.

You can leave the Dales Way from here, down a steep, stepped path through the woods to Otley town centre for return transport. Otherwise head along the outside of the walls along the ridge summit, through mature woods above and behind the former York Gate Quarry, now a car park.

But for the energetic campaigning work in the 1970s of Otley architect, conservationist and cartographer of the Dales Way, the late Arthur Gemmell, this quarry would have broken through the skyline with disastrous consequences for the natural ecosystem and landscape.

The path eventually reaches a stile and crosses a field to join York Gate Lane beyond Woodland Farm. A section of unavoidable road walking follows, downhill to Woods Farm, turning left at the first then right at the second crossroads, to reach the Chevin Inn below. To the right of the inn the Dales Way follows a path which curves down over stiles and through fields before turning left along a track. Turn right again at the next crossing of paths to reach and then follow the railway line above Menston, crossing the railway and main A6938 by the bridge to walk along Station Road to Menston Station.

A bit of suburban walking follows now, taking the enclosed footpath alongside the railway station and railway, keeping ahead at the end of the path to walk along Fairfax Road to its end, then left along Brierly Lane past the church, turning right along Main Street. As it bends left keep ahead along Bleach Mill Lane, which becomes a sunken, stony track, with open views. It leads behind the old bleach mill (now a private house), ahead through

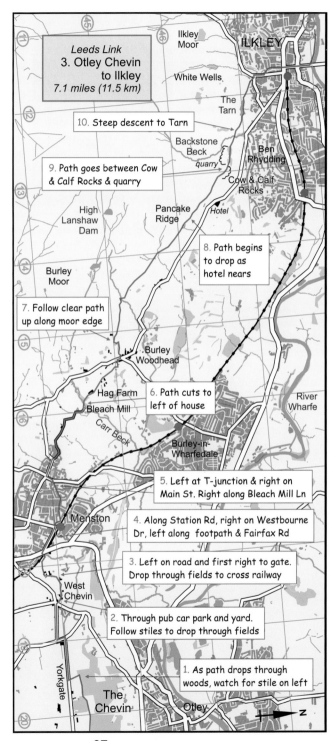

Leeds Link
3. Otley Chevin to Ilkley
7.1 miles (11.5 km)

Ilkley Moor

ILKLEY

White Wells

The Tarn

10. Steep descent to Tarn

Backstone Beck

quarry

Ben Rhydding

9. Path goes between Cow & Calf Rocks & quarry

Cow & Calf Rocks

High Lanshaw Dam

Pancake Ridge

Hotel

8. Path begins to drop as hotel nears

Burley Moor

7. Follow clear path up along moor edge

Burley Woodhead

Hag Farm

Bleach Mill

Carr Beck

6. Path cuts to left of house

River Wharfe

Burley-in-Wharfedale

5. Left at T-junction & right on Main St. Right along Bleach Mill Ln

Menston

4. Along Station Rd, right on Westbourne Dr, left along footpath & Fairfax Rd

3. Left on road and first right to gate. Drop through fields to cross railway

West Chevin

2. Through pub car park and yard. Follow stiles to drop through fields

1. As path drops through woods, watch for stile on left

Yorkgate

The Chevin

Otley

stiles, below Hag Farm and behind the Hermit Inn, then through fields and left up a house drive before reaching Moor Road at Burley Woodhead. Turn right, but cross almost immediately to where a footpath, signed, leads onto Burley Moor opposite the crossroads from Burley-in-Wharfedale.

The most dramatic section of the Leeds Dales Way Link now follows. The path,

Sculpture, Chevin Forest Park

clearly marked, climbs steeply up through a shallow moorside ravine and twists its way to the right, above Barks Crag onto the moor edge. From this point onwards, path finding is relatively easy.

This part of the route is shared with the Ebor Way from York and is a classic moor edge ridge walk, ascending over the summit of Stead Crag, with increasingly fine views up the valley, and to the south over the expanse of heather, peat and rough grassland that covers Burley and later Ilkley Moors.

You eventually reach the Cow and Calf rocks with car parks below you and pub and restaurant opposite. There is a bewildering

choice of paths here, but if you maintain the general direction there will be little problem.

Head behind these iconic rocks to locate the path between the rocks and the quarry which eventually descends into the shallow gorge formed by Backstone Beck, where a footbridge leads to a steep path up the gill side to Ilkley's Tarn. This has been transformed to look more like a Victorian town park pond than a moorland tarn, but enjoys a fine location.

Take the path from the end of the Tarn which crosses by the little shelter down to Darwin Gardens, at the far corner of which a little bridge leads into yet another wooded gorge. Follow the path down. If you keep to the left side of the stream across the entrance to the former Ilkley Spa (later the college, now apartments), a short path takes you into Linnburn Mews. At the end of the mews and across Queens Road, a metal gate on the right leads into Mill Gill Gardens. Follow the beckside path to the centre of Ilkley — trains and buses to the right, ahead an excellent choice of cafes and pubs. The "mainline" Dales Way starts from the riverside at the Old Bridge, a quarter of a mile away.

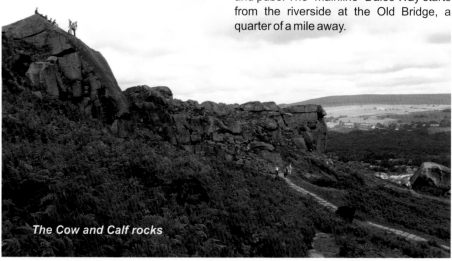

The Cow and Calf rocks

The Bradford Link

12½ miles (20 km)

The Dales Way Bradford Link was devised by the Bradford Group of the Ramblers Association in 1970. This route initially began in Shipley at the edge of the Bradford conurbation, but Bradford Council countryside service, recognising the value of the Dales Way to the city of Bradford, has recently developed an extension of the route direct from the city centre through Bradford Dale to Shipley. This four mile addition may be mainly urban in character but has real charm, and some nice surprises.

Begin by Bradford Cathedral, reasonably accessible from Forster Square station, behind the Broadway shopping centre.

The route starts at the large metal gates leading up to Bradford Cathedral. Turn north to reach and ascend stone steps on the right. Walk uphill on the paved path to Stott Hill. Bear left here, crossing diagonally into Captain Street opposite, following it to reach Bolton Road near the Corn Dolly pub. Turn right here up Bolton Road to the traffic lights on the Shipley-Airedale Road.

Spinks Well

Left here to the pelican crossing, then turn right, crossing the main road to rejoin Bolton Road on the opposite side. Continue up Bolton Road for 250 metres before going left down Lawson Street. Turn right at the bottom of this short street into Coleman Street. At its end, a kissing gate leads into Boars Well Urban Wildlife Reserve.

This little linear nature reserve lies on a south-west facing slope and is a popular place to enjoy wild flowers, butterflies and birds. Among the scattered woodland and hedgerows are hawthorn, willow, blackthorn, birch and rowan, as well as well established garden escapees dogwood and buddleia. Kestrels nest nearby and can often be seen hunting over the hillside. This woodland is a reminder of how green Bradford Dale was before Bradford became a world centre of the wool industry, with canal, railway and trunk road covering this once green Pennine valley. Bradford Beck once flowed freely through this little valley to join the River Aire at Shipley, but is now mostly concealed in culverts, though the walk passes open-air sections.

Follow the path through the reserve along the hillside. Ignore the path leading off to the left but continue on into Kings Road. Right here to the traffic lights at the junction with Queens Road. Cross (with care) to walk up the left-hand side of the continuation of Kings Road to where it meets Bolton Lane. Turn left here, crossing Kingsley Avenue near the bottom of the hill, taking the next turn right along a narrow unsurfaced road, Hollin Close Lane. This bears right up a slight incline to the gateway of a house. Take the narrow footpath on the right between the back of the house and newer houses on the right.

The area between here and Livingstone Road at Bolton Woods is subject to development in the coming years, so expect some changes and watch out for Dales Way markers.

Follow the path through metal bollards, climbing steeply uphill towards trees where you join another path by some new housing. Go left here onto a cobbled, then tarmac enclosed path, up a slight incline. Beyond a gate, bear right on a path up to cross Poplars Park Road. Head uphill on a signed bridleway, passing some metal gates. Turn sharp left through a walkers gate and follow the path, keeping left at a

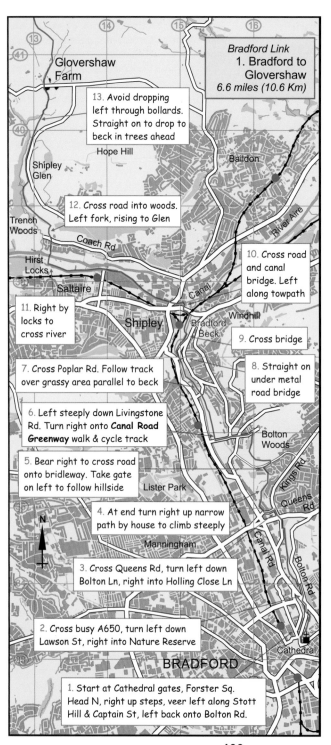

Glovershaw Farm

Bradford Link
1. Bradford to Glovershaw
6.6 miles (10.6 Km)

13. Avoid dropping left through bollards. Straight on to drop to beck in trees ahead

Hope Hill

Baildon

Shipley Glen

River Aire

Trench Woods

12. Cross road into woods. Left fork, rising to Glen

Coach Rd

Hirst Locks

10. Cross road and canal bridge. Left along towpath

Saltaire

Canal

11. Right by locks to cross river

Shipley

Bradford Beck

Windhill

9. Cross bridge

7. Cross Poplar Rd. Follow track over grassy area parallel to beck

8. Straight on under metal road bridge

6. Left steeply down Livingstone Rd. Turn right onto **Canal Road Greenway** walk & cycle track

Bolton Woods

5. Bear right to cross road onto bridleway. Take gate on left to follow hillside

Lister Park

Kings Rd

4. At end turn right up narrow path by house to climb steeply

N

Queens Rd

Manningham

Canal Rd

3. Cross Queens Rd, turn left down Bolton Ln, right into Holling Close Ln

Bolton Rd

2. Cross busy A650, turn left down Lawson St, right into Nature Reserve

Cathedral

BRADFORD

1. Start at Cathedral gates, Forster Sq. Head N, right up steps, veer left along Stott Hill & Captain St, left back onto Bolton Rd.

fork to follow the hillside contour to a stile just beneath a small copse. Continue along the contours of the hillside, curving gently right to a kissing gate.

Fine views from here across the semi-urban landscape of Bradford Dale, still dominated by fine old mill buildings, with Manningham Mills a notable landmark.

From the kissing gate the definitive path curves right to squeeze into Chestnut Grove by a house, but it's easier to follow the clear track ahead, diagonally left downhill. Keep ahead to Livingstone Road. Turn left here, descending past the primary school and New Vic public house. Cross Gaisby Lane and continue downhill towards the busy A6037, turning right just before the main road to join the Canal Road Greenway - a new tarmac track for walkers and cyclists which shadows the Bradford Beck to its left. Continue on to cross Poplar Road, following the Greenway along the large grassy area opposite. The Greenway eventually passes underneath a metal road bridge with the Beck still down to the left.

Here again the area is due to be developed in the future, so once again watch for Dales Way markers. Continue along the Greenway and at a fork bear left to cross the beck at a bridge. Continue north, with the beck now down to the right and Shipley railway station to the left. Keeping the railway on the left, you eventually emerge under two railway arches to the cobbled entrance road into Shipley Station.

Unless you are catching a train, go onto Leeds Road and a pelican crossing by the lights. Cross, turning left towards concrete bollards ahead. Turn right into the (signed) path leading to a footbridge over the Leeds-Liverpool Canal. Cross, turning left to follow the towpath past the Shipley canal wharfs for a mile and a quarter to Saltaire.

The industrial village of Saltaire, designated a U N E S C O world heritage site in 2001, was created in the 1860s by the great wool and alpaca magnate Sir Titus Salt: a model village served by the Leeds-Liverpool Canal and the Midland Railway, yet away from the smoke and pollution

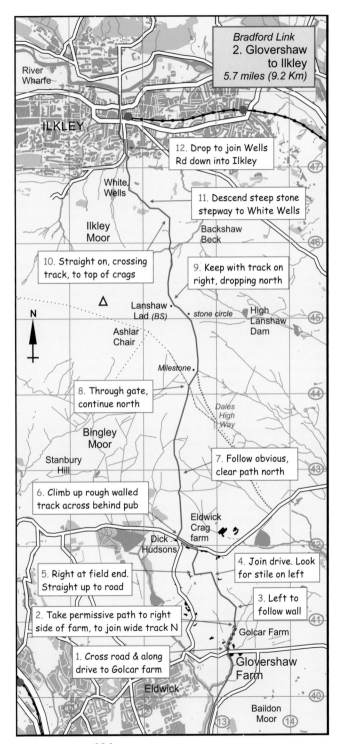

Bradford Link
2. Glovershaw to Ilkley
5.7 miles (9.2 Km)

River Wharfe

ILKLEY

12. Drop to join Wells Rd down into Ilkley

White Wells

11. Descend steep stone stepway to White Wells

Ilkley Moor

Backshaw Beck

10. Straight on, crossing track, to top of crags

9. Keep with track on right, dropping north

N

Lanshaw Lad *(BS)*

stone circle

High Lanshaw Dam

Ashlar Chair

Milestone

8. Through gate, continue north

Dales High Way

Bingley Moor

Stanbury Hill

7. Follow obvious, clear path north

6. Climb up rough walled track across behind pub

Eldwick Crag farm

Dick Hudsons

4. Join drive. Look for stile on left

5. Right at field end. Straight up to road

3. Left to follow wall

2. Take permissive path to right side of farm, to join wide track N

Golcar Farm

1. Cross road & along drive to Golcar farm

Glovershaw Farm

Eldwick

Baildon Moor

47
46
45
44
43
42
41
40
13
14

101

of central Bradford. It is a magnificent example of 19th century town planning with fine village hall, church, school and park. Salts Mill now has a superb art gallery, closely associated with the works of the celebrated Bradford-born artist David Hockney. There are shops, cafes and toilets in the village.

Continue along the towpath to Hirst Wood Lock, the first canal lock after Saltaire. Take the gap through the stone wall right, go down the steps and cross the footbridge over the River Aire. Continue straight ahead along the path past Bowland and Glenwood Avenue, keeping ahead past the bus stop and over Coach Road to reach an unsurfaced bridleway straight ahead. Follow this uphill to take the left fork into the attractive oak woods of Trench Woods and Shipley Glen. Where the path eventually reaches the top, turn left along the edge of the glen.

Shipley Glen was a thriving place of resort for Bradford people in Victorian times, its popular funfair served by a small cable tramway which still runs in the summer months, and is a good starting point for many countryside walks. Exhibitions of the archaeology, local and natural history of both Shipley Glen and nearby Baildon Moor can be seen at the Bracken Hall countryside centre on Glen Road.

Follow the wide well-trodden path parallel to Glen Road. Where the path divides, just before reaching the two concrete bollards ahead, take the narrow track which bears slightly to the right. Walk straight ahead to follow the grassy path through bracken, eventually passing old quarry workings on your left, just beyond which the track goes down an incline and crosses towards trees ahead. The path continues straight ahead, alongside Glovershaw Beck, to cross a footbridge over the beck before turning left over a second bridge to pass below Glovershaw Farm and on to the very busy Glovershaw Lane.

Cross to walk up the driveway opposite, leading past Willowfield and up to Golcar Farm. Where the drive turns left into the farmyard, continue straight ahead to where the footpath divides to bear left on a short permissive diversion to avoid the farmyard. Go through the bridleway gate, turn right after only a short distance, then immediately left to follow a wide grassy track out of the farm complex.

Take the stile on the side of a field gate and continue up to the next gate. Do not go through this second gate but turn sharp left to go through the adjacent gate, still following the track, with the stone wall on your left, to another field gate ahead. Cross the adjoining stile and continue straight across this field, before bearing slightly to the right, past a wooden electricity pole, towards the field gate ahead. Keep ahead along the wall/fence to a gate into a drive by two detached houses.

Walk 150 metres along this drive to a stile in the wall on your left. It leads to a path which runs alongside the wall on your left, crossing a very wet section of field heading towards a stile at the bottom left hand corner near Toils Farm. Do not cross here but turn right up the field, following the stone wall on your left. Where the wall turns sharp left, continue straight ahead, bearing slightly to the right to a stile. Turn left onto the very busy Otley Road, walking along the narrow verge for 300 metres by Eldwick Crag to Dick Hudson's public house.

This popular Victorian public house was originally called The Fleece, but took its name from Richard or Dick Hudson who was landlord between 1850 and 1878, a time when workers from the thriving busy mills of Shipley and Bingley came up here. Many walked the ancient packhorse way over Rombalds Moor to Ilkley at weekends and holiday times, and called in Dick Hudson's for a pint of beer and one of the inn's famous yorkshire puddings on their way home.

From the far side of the pub buildings, cross Otley Road (with care) to join the well-walked footpath at a narrow gate. This leads into a path between walls which soon begins to climb steeply past Spy Hill with a magnificent view from here down into Airedale and across the South Pennines, before descending to cross boggy areas around Weecher Mouth and Hog Hill Flat. You then follow a fine paved section of medieval packhorse way, heading due north onto Bingley Moor. This path is so well known and well inscribed into the moorland, it hardly needs description, but care is needed over the occasional boggy stretches.

After about a mile you reach and cross the stone boundary wall at a stile and enter Burley Moor.

The whole gritstone massif between Airedale and Wharfedale constitutes Rombalds Moor, but each adjacent township still has its own section of named moor, where, in times past, freeholders held grazing rights.

The path continues to ascend across a wild and desolate area of rough grazing and peat and heather moorland. Eventually the route levels out along the summit ridge, about 380 metres (1,300 feet) above sea level. As the path bends slightly left, look for a small prehistoric stone circle in the heather to the right.

This is the Twelve Apostles – a small circle of standing stones, almost certainly early Bronze Age in origin, though sadly the stones have been vandalised and moved over the years. Nevertheless this is a wonderful viewpoint, the place where the essentially harsh semi-industrial landscape of the South Pennines yields to the softer, more verdant Yorkshire Dales as you look down into mid-Wharfedale. Across to the east is Otley Chevin, then Almscliffe Crag with the towns of Otley and Burley below. Beyond is Denton Moor within the Nidderdale AONB (see Harrogate link), further west Beamsley Beacon and the Yorkshire Dales National Park, and as you walk on, the roofs and spires and railway of Ilkley emerge in a vast, living panorama below you.

Walk on to the small cairn and stone column known as the Lanshaw Lad.

This is an ancient boundary stone and marks the point where the Dales Way enters Ilkley Moor, which has become perhaps the world's most famous moor thanks to the popularity of a Victorian song, an anthem whose grim humour is also a celebration of the stoic character of Yorkshire people themselves. Ilkley Moor, owned by the people of Ilkley and Bradford, is also an archaeological treasure house, noted for its cup and ring marked rocks, stone circles, and the famous Swastika Stone, rock art which dates from the early Bronze Age.

Enjoy continuous spectacular views as the path descends quite steeply, with board walks in places, as well as paved sections to reduce erosion. Soon you begin to descend rough, and at times quite steep, stone steps. Care is needed, as the path, now incised deeply into the hillside, curves through the rocky outcrops of Ilkley Crags.

As you approach the little complex of white-painted buildings and pine trees at White Wells below, take a diversion down the steps on the right to visit this little 18th century spa building where invalids once suffered the freezing water "cure" in icy plunge pools, one of which can still be visited, if not sampled. Tea and light refreshments are available here at weekends and holiday periods.

A steep, stepped path leads directly down the slope from White Wells towards the centre of Ilkley. The pleasantest way to minimise street walking is to descend to the town centre via Darwin Gardens and Mill Gill – see the route description in the Leeds Link. Frequent train services leave Ilkley Station back to Shipley and Bradford.

Ilkley Moor and the Cow & Calf Hotel (above). Haverah Park (below).

Swinsty Reservoir

The Harrogate Link

16½ miles (26½ km)

The Harrogate Dales Way Link path is an especially splendid walk in its own right, crossing as it does the southern heart of the Nidderdale Area of Outstanding Natural Beauty, an area of the eastern Dales which, though it does not have national park status, is scenically, geographically and culturally an integral part of the Yorkshire Dales.

The route owes its concept and origin to the Harrogate Group of the Ramblers Association and in particular to one of its founding fathers, Corrie Gaunt of Harrogate, one of the great footpath campaigners of the north of England, who was for many years footpath secretary of the West Riding RA.

The present route between Harrogate and the start of the Dales Way in Ilkley is actually the second Harrogate Dales Way Link. The original link through Haverah Park, across the Washburn Valley via Blubberhouses and Barden Fell up to the Rocking Stone and

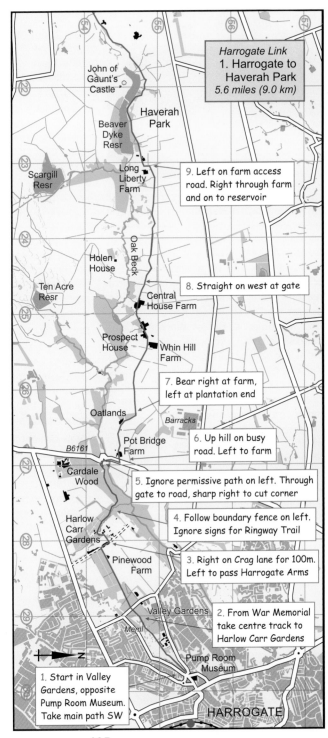

Harrogate Link
1. Harrogate to Haverah Park
5.6 miles (9.0 km)

John of Gaunt's Castle

Haverah Park

Beaver Dyke Resr

Scargill Resr

Long Liberty Farm

9. Left on farm access road. Right through farm and on to reservoir

Oak Beck

Holen House

Ten Acre Resr

Central House Farm

8. Straight on west at gate

Prospect House

Whin Hill Farm

7. Bear right at farm, left at plantation end

Oatlands

Barracks

B6161

Pot Bridge Farm

6. Up hill on busy road. Left to farm

Cardale Wood

5. Ignore permissive path on left. Through gate to road, sharp right to cut corner

Harlow Carr Gardens

4. Follow boundary fence on left. Ignore signs for Ringway Trail

Pinewood Farm

3. Right on Crag lane for 100m. Left to pass Harrogate Arms

Valley Gardens

Menal

2. From War Memorial take centre track to Harlow Carr Gardens

Pump Room Museum

1. Start in Valley Gardens, opposite Pump Room Museum. Take main path SW

HARROGATE

The Pump Room Museum

Until the late 17th century and the discovery of the many mineral springs and wells, *Hargate* was a hamlet close to the bustling market town of Knaresborough. But by the late 18th century the fashionable spa of **Harrogate** had developed, attracting the rich and infirm from all over England to drink or bathe in the healing - if somewhat smelly - sulphurous waters. Several original wells with their heavy iron lids can still be seen in the Valley Gardens, in what is still known as Low Harrogate. This park and the pine woods of its hinterland now form a beautiful green corridor leading from the busy centre of the modern town of Harrogate, the perfect starting point for the Harrogate Dales Way Link.

across Bolton Park to join the Dales Way at Bolton Abbey, was a superb route. However, it had to be abandoned as the official Dales Way for slightly bizarre reasons. Much of the route crossed public access land over the Chatsworth estate, who welcomed it. But as the route used permissive paths, not public rights of way, the estate had the full legal right to close the route at times of shooting or when there was a fire risk. Unfortunately Ordnance Survey show approved long-distance paths as a series of small green diamonds, which many walkers also assume, wrongly, mean a public right of way. This could obviously result in misunderstanding, conflict and even danger to the public. When asked to change the colour of the diamonds from green to red (as permissive paths are usually shown) to obviate this problem over land where no highway rights existed, Ordnance Survey indicated they couldn't change the colour they used for long-distance paths and therefore removed the whole of the Harrogate Dales Way Link from their maps.

Rather than fight a lost cause, Harrogate Ramblers took a sensible step – to move the Dales Way Link and use an equally fine route, this time going via Timble and Denton Moors direct to Ilkley. The older route still survives and can be walked at all times when the moor is open for public

access. The new route has fewer restrictions, and importantly can be shown on new editions of OS maps. Harrogate Ramblers has already done an excellent job of surveying and waymarking the route throughout.

Both routes are identical as far as the Washburn Valley. The official start of the Harrogate Link is the entrance to the Valley Gardens, opposite the Pump Room Museum. Take the main path through the gardens, bearing right away from the stream and below the pavilion.

Keep straight ahead past flower beds and wells, below the Royal Baths Hospital, heading for the woods ahead. Make sure you take the centre track from the war memorial signed to Harlow Carr Gardens, passing through pine woods, taking a left fork (signed) to reach and cross the busy Harlow Moor Road. Continue along the tarmac path along the edge of the woods to emerge on Crag Lane, almost opposite the celebrated RHS gardens of Harlow Carr. Turn right here for 100 metres to where a path, signed, follows the fence around the northern perimeter of the gardens, past the Harrogate Arms pub, continuing right, along the boundary fence and down into the beautiful wooded valley formed by Oak Beck. Keep right at a fork and follow the path along the top of the valley towards the cottage at Cardale Wood.

Ignore the permissive path on the left and keep straight ahead through the gate past the cottage (this is the public path) into the B6161 Beckwithshaw Road.

Take care here to avoid fast moving traffic, and head downhill (look for the path on the right which cuts across the bend in the road) to cross the old stone arched bridge over Oak Beck before taking the first track on the left past Pot Bridge Farm.

You are now entering Haverah Park. Go towards Oatlands Farm, bearing up the slope alongside a small plantation, at the end of which the path swings left, heading due west following a wall above a series of sloping fields rising from the shallow valley formed by Oak Beck. Keep past Whin Hill and Prospect House Farms, following the track through the farmyards. Continue straight ahead alongside walls, easy

walking, towards Long Liberty Farm. Turn left here on the farm access road, turning right through the farm to join the path above the reservoir, soon passing scattered woodlands above Beaver Dyke Reservoirs. Across the valley is a low mound with stone ruins known as John of Gaunt's Castle.

This mound is reputed to be the hunting lodge of John of Gaunt, Duke of Lancaster, and probably dates from the 14th century when Haverah Park was part of the hunting Forest of Knaresborough.

From the Corrie Gaunt seat, descend to the green lane which runs along an old earthwork, possibly a part of the old forest boundary, known as Bank Slack. The path crosses below Bank Slack Farm, descending to the left, over shallow streams and stiles, to emerge by cottages

The Battle for Haverah Park

A small memorial bench opposite John of Gaunt's Castle carries a Ramblers' memorial to the late Corrie Gaunt, lifetime campaigner for public rights of way. In 1957 a number of rights of way were claimed by the Ramblers' Association through the 2,000 acres of Haverah Park. These were opposed by the local water board in whose catchment area and over whose land the footpaths went. However, the then West Riding Ramblers' assistant footpath secretary Corrie Gaunt was able to put a case to the County Council, with evidence, much of which was collected at a local public meeting he had organised. Corrie quoted evidence going back to the 17th century, citing for example a court case in which one William Simpson was accused of an offence because he "did stoppe a common foote way in Long Lees and Upper Close" in the park, proving beyond doubt that in 1667 at least a public footpath did indeed exist.

One elderly man recalled that his

grandparents had kept the local Sun Inn at Norwood at the edge of the park, and on fine Sundays in his childhood he could remember a large number of people walking there along the disputed path from Harrogate, for a one shilling dinner of carved roast meat and yorkshire pudding.

But the cat was truly let out of the bag when a farmer, asked by the Harrogate water engineer to state that he had turned ramblers back on the disputed paths, wrote: "I must write the truth about this right of way through Haverah Park. I lived at Long Liberty Farm for nine years, and I can truthfully say we never turned any ramblers back as long as they kept to the Roman Road and did not go looking for mushrooms or rabbiting."

This overwhelming evidence was duly accepted by the County Council. The paths are now busy with ramblers at any time of the week or year, many walking the Harrogate Dales Way Link which could not have existed without the painstaking work of Corrie Gaunt.

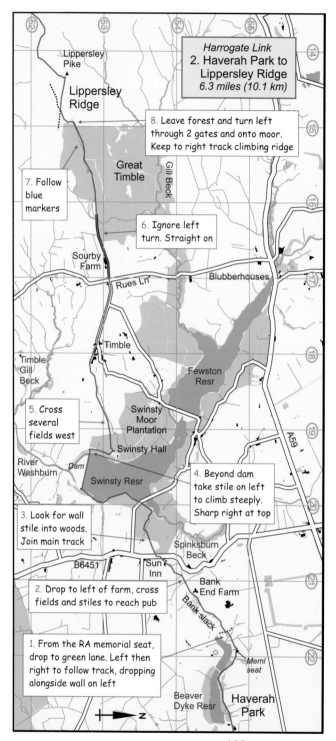

Harrogate Link
2. Haverah Park to Lippersley Ridge
6.3 miles (10.1 km)

Lippersley Pike

Lippersley Ridge

Great Timble

Gill Beck

8. Leave forest and turn left through 2 gates and onto moor. Keep to right track climbing ridge

7. Follow blue markers

6. Ignore left turn. Straight on

Sourby Farm

Rues Ln

Blubberhouses

Timble

Timble Gill Beck

Fewston Resr

5. Cross several fields west

Swinsty Moor Plantation

Swinsty Hall

River Washburn

Dam

Swinsty Resr

A59

4. Beyond dam take stile on left to climb steeply. Sharp right at top

3. Look for wall stile into woods. Join main track

Spinksburn Beck

B6451

Sun Inn

Bank End Farm

2. Drop to left of farm, cross fields and stiles to reach pub

Bank slack

1. From the RA memorial seat, drop to green lane. Left then right to follow track, dropping alongside wall on left

Meml seat

Beaver Dyke Resr

Haverah Park

N

known as Bramelane onto the B6451 road by the Sun Inn.

Cross the road, turning left for 80 metres to where a path on the right, signed, leads across a couple of fields before entering and descending through woodland into the Washburn Valley. At the bottom of the wood join a narrow enclosed way which emerges alongside a side pool of Swinsty Reservoir.

The Dales Way follows the reservoir edge, crossing the Fewston road. Turn left here to follow the path along and around the edge of the reservoir, heading for Swinsty Dam embankment.

Cross the dam. A little care is needed at the far end here to locate the stile on the left across which a path climbs steeply up to another stile, leading, sharp right, into the woods. Turn left after 200 metres, to go round the back of Swinsty Hall (a fine Jacobean house hidden in the woods). Keep ahead to the gateway leading out of the woods to take the path, not clear on the ground, through fields and gates, which eventually enters a walled track. This leads past High Field Farm to the village of Timble – look for an opening on the right to the Timble Inn and village centre.

Timble village lies only a few miles from urban West Yorkshire yet is deeply rural, its development restricted because of the need of the former Leeds Corporation Water Board to reduce development in nearby water catchment areas and thereby minimise potential pollution. The Timble Inn, long a favourite haunt of walkers, but closed for a number of years, has recently reopened as a restaurant.

Link paths heading north out of Timble lead to Blubberhouses for buses back to Harrogate.

But to continue to Ilkley, take the main lane due west out of Timble, passing the crossroads to reach and cross the main Blubberhouses road (more fast traffic). Continue along the quiet Sourby Lane opposite, which soon becomes an unsurfaced track, keeping straight ahead at the junction to head past Red Gates and into the centre of the dense Timble Ings plantation, consisting mainly of

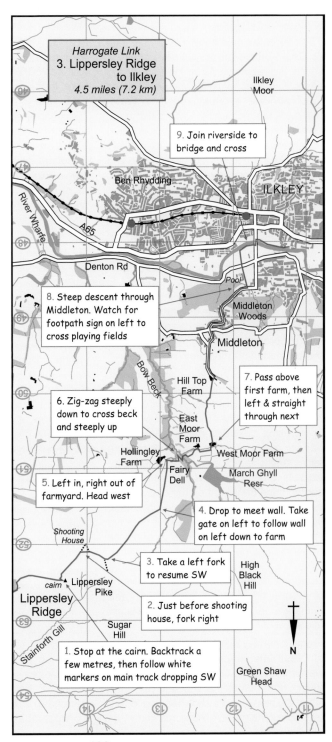

Harrogate Link
3. Lippersley Ridge to Ilkley
4.5 miles (7.2 km)

Ilkley Moor

9. Join riverside to bridge and cross

Ben Rhydding

ILKLEY

River Wharfe

A65

Denton Rd

Pool

8. Steep descent through Middleton. Watch for footpath sign on left to cross playing fields

Middleton Woods

Middleton

Bow Beck

Hill Top Farm

7. Pass above first farm, then left & straight through next

6. Zig-zag steeply down to cross beck and steeply up

East Moor Farm

Hollingley Farm

West Moor Farm

Fairy Dell

March Ghyll Resr

5. Left in, right out of farmyard. Head west

4. Drop to meet wall. Take gate on left to follow wall on left down to farm

Shooting House

3. Take a left fork to resume SW

High Black Hill

cairn Lippersley Pike

Lippersley Ridge

2. Just before shooting house, fork right

Stainforth Gill

Sugar Hill

1. Stop at the cairn. Backtrack a few metres, then follow white markers on main track dropping SW

N

Green Shaw Head

109

larch, spruce and pine.

This afforested area known as Timble Ings or Great Timble forms, with the chain of Washburn reservoirs, their foreshores and timbered slopes, part of Yorkshire Water's Washburndale estates. Yorkshire Water manages the estates for water catchment, timber production, wildlife conservation and public access. A series of popular well-waymarked trails offers circular walks and some cycle and equestrian routes from well-screened car parks close by.

Follow the blue waymarks into the centre of the forest, past small ponds, keeping straight ahead at all junctions through bridle gates. At the end of the forest the path swings left to join an ancient path known as High Badgergate. Turn right to follow this path along Lippersley Ridge, a low ridge crossing the heather and peat hags of Denton Moor, past an old Forest of Knaresborough boundary stone, towards the low mound of Lippersley Pike ahead.

Badgergate literally means a *pedlars' road*. This was a part of an ancient packhorse way between Halifax, Keighley and Knaresborough, used by itinerant peddlers or travelling salesmen (hence the verb *to badger*, or *pester*), who visited outlying farms and villages as well as the major markets offering their wares which they carried huge distances on their persons or by pony. Lippersley Pike has a large cairn built on what is probably a tumulus or grave mound, possibly Bronze Age in origin as evidenced by a number of cup-marked rocks in the vicinity. It is a splendid viewpoint in clear weather, with the summit of Beamsley Beacon lying within the boundary of the national park, straight ahead.

From Lippersley Pike look for a narrow path on your left which heads due south-westwards across Denton Moor. Take care to fork right before the shooting hut, then left at the next fork. You are heading for the wall above the green enclosures known as Hollingley Intake below.

At the wall corner ignore the stile ahead but go though the gate on the left. Follow the wall down three fields towards Hollingley Farm to the gate at the bottom of the third field. Turn left through the gate but then immediately sharp right through a second adjacent gate. Follow this path down as it bears left through bracken and into woodland, twisting down to the left again then zigzagging to the right and left once more to a tiny footbridge into what is still known as Fairy Dell – a once popular walk in Victorian times from Ilkley.

The path now climbs out of the valley ahead, going past and above East Moor Farm and then left at the gate through the farmyard at West Moor Farm.

Walk straight ahead on the farm access road now, as it descends gently to join the lane from Hunger Hill at Hill Top Farm. Continue due south, down the lane towards the tiny village of Middleton, on the very edge of Ilkley yet inexplicably part of Harrogate District, some 16 miles away. Fork right through the hamlet. You emerge at the top of Curley Hill, an avenue of handsome houses which forms Ilkley's most northerly suburb.

Easy walking now, downhill, as the road curves past Middleton and Stubham Woods. Look for the sign on the left which indicates a path through a gap stile into a narrow strip of trees which emerges in playing fields by Ilkley's popular lido and swimming pool. Straight ahead here, crossing the road by the pool car park and entrance to join the path at a gap leading past rugby grounds to the riverside. Turn right alongside the river to Ilkley's Middleton Bridge, crossing the bridge and walking up to the traffic lights. Straight ahead up Brook Street to the centre of Ilkley for cafes, pubs, shops, toilets, and a choice of frequent trains to Leeds (for Harrogate) or Bradford, or less regular but more direct buses to Harrogate.

References & notes

The first point of call for anyone planning to walk the Dales Way is the *Dales Way Association (DWA)*:

website - **www.dalesway.org**

or contact by mail; The Dales Way Association, PO Box 334, Shipley, BD18 9DZ.

The DWA was set up in 1991 to promote, support and maintain the Dales Way long-distance path. Membership is open to all who have walked, or plan to walk, the Dales Way or simply care about its future. In 2013 the DWA was registered as a small Charity (registered with the Inland Revenue, number: XT3838). A three-year membership currently costs £18 per individual, £24 for a family. Membership is primarily a way of supporting the work of the association

The Dales Way Association website features the latest news about the Dales Way. It also carries details of: maps & guide books, baggage transfer and accommodation booking services, link routes to the Dales Way, updates to the route, facilities & places of interest, public transport available, and an accommodation list including hotels, guest houses, bed & breakfast, youth hostels, bunk barns & campsites.

Another useful source of information on accommodation providers can be found on the Sherpa Van Project website: **www.thedalesway.co.uk**

Additional information about this book, including any updates and an interactive OS map of the Dales Way route, can be found at the Skyware website: **www.skyware.co.uk/dalesway.htm**

(All websites referenced June 2013).

Photo Credits

Colin Speakman: p5, p8 (bottom), p10 (both), p12 (bottom), p14, p18, p28 (top), p33 (top left & top right), p50, p66 (both), p87, p89 (top right).

Dorian Speakman: p16 (top – both), p37 (bottom left), p104 (bottom).

Frank Sanderson: p12 (top).

James Cropper plc: p80 (all).

Skyware: Front cover, back cover, title page, p8 (top), p9, p11, p13, p16 (bottom), p17,

Alex McManus, DWA footpath officer (left), & Colin Speakman, DWA chairman (right), relax at the end of the Dales Way, 2009.

p22, p25, p27, p28 (all except top), p30, p33 (mid left & bottom), p34, p35, p37 (top, bottom right), p41 (both), p43, p51, p55 (all), p56, p57, p62, p63, p68 (all), p70, p71, p75 (both), p77, , p82, p89 (top left & bottom), p92 (all), p94, p98 (both), p99, p104 (top & middle), p106, p111, p112.

Acknowledgements

Thanks to Tony Grogan for producing the strip maps and designing the book.

For checking the maps and route details we thank Alex McManus, DWA footpath officer, and also the Rights of Way officers for the Yorkshire Dales National Park, the Lake District National Park, Cumbria County Council, North Yorkshire County Council, Bradford Metropolitan District Council and Leeds City Council.

For information in the Dales Way Planner, thanks to Chris Grogan, DWA secretary.

For proof reading thanks to Bridget Izod, with help from Chris Grogan.

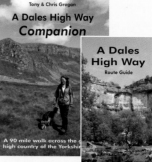

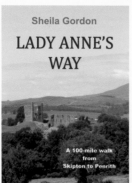

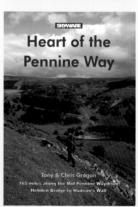